# PLATOON LEADER

# A MEMOIR
# OF COMMAND
# IN COMBAT

## JAMES R. MCDONOUGH

**Look for these gripping true stories
of courage and combat in Vietnam:**

NOT GOING HOME ALONE
*A Marine's Story*
by James J. Kirschke

PATHFINDER
*First In, Last Out*
by Richard R. Burns

13 CENT KILLERS
*The 5th Marine Snipers in Vietnam*
by John J. Culbertson

GUNS UP!
by Johnnie M. Clark

Ballantine / Del Rey /
Fawcett / Ivy

ISBN 0-89141-800-8

U.S. $6.99/Canada $10.99

EAN

# "ENORMOUSLY VIVID AND COMPELLING . . .

[This book] pays welcome tribute to both the American soldiers and the Truong Lam villagers who suffered and died. . . . McDonough not only expresses his feelings of responsibility for his men and for the villagers they defended but also lays bare his personal fears and his realization of the fine line between rational leadership and irrational killing."

*—Booklist*

"McDonough spent five months with his platoon; in those five months, he learned a lot about tactics, weapons, and—most important—leadership. He learned to conquer his own fear, and, after that, how to control the mob instinct that gnaws at the inside of any army. . . . *Platoon Leader* is an honest guide to the touchy art of setting limits on violence."

*—St. Louis Post-Dispatch*

"Extraordinary glimpses of the chancy and hard life of the young men who actually did the fighting in Vietnam . . . For anyone interested in the daily grind of the combat soldier, this is a true portrayal."

*—The San Diego Union*

"McDonough is unusual: a military analyst who helped reshape the army's thinking . . . and a noteworthy author."

*—The Wall Street Journal*

*Please turn the page for more reviews. . . .*

# "A CLASSIC ACCOUNT OF SMALL-UNIT LEADERSHIP DURING WAR . . .

The experiences related in the book reinforce what we learn: disciplined soldiers will fight well, win, and survive to fight again. . . . McDonough's story is also about the American soldier. The soldiers of his platoon were not Rambos or John Waynes. There were tough guys, scared guys, and laid-back soldiers. They were also men who fought for their friends, and for their country."
—*Armor Magazine*

"After writing my book on my World War II experiences, *Company Commander*, I eagerly awaited someone doing for the platoon leader what I had tried to do for the company commander. . . . Now my search at long last is over. With *Platoon Leader*, James McDonough has done it all and done it in a way that can hardly be beat. . . . The author writes without bravado, with intense honesty, and, most especially, with telling introspection about his emotions and reactions. . . . Jim McDonough's story is what leadership at the foxhole level is all about."
—CHARLES B. MACDONALD
*Army Magazine*

"Jim McDonough has written a superb book about leadership in combat. Although he disclaims any purpose other than to tell the story of a U.S. Army platoon leader in combat, his book is more than just a war story. It is a book about the U.S. soldier. . . . It is a book that every combat arms leader should read."
—*Infantry Magazine*

# "AN EXCELLENT BOOK ABOUT WAR.

We learn a lot about what the Vietnam War was like and about how it was for the American units, and a little about the Vietnamese, its chief victims. But above all, perhaps, we learn about the Middle American Soul. . . . [McDonough's] descriptions of some of his soldiers . . . are vivid. They are interlaced with a low-key patriotic assertion of the nobility of soldiering and of battle itself, of national interest and obedience, and of camaraderie, bravery, and fortitude."

—*The Jerusalem Post*

"A first-person account of the rigors and challenges that a young army lieutenant faces during his first six months in Vietnam . . . This is a factual book about war, young men conquering daily fears in the elements, knowing that if they are exposed long enough, they are challenging the odds."

—*Los Angeles Times*

"The author spells out, among other things, the process—sometimes humorous, often painful—through which a neophyte fresh out of training becomes a combat veteran. . . . Most important of all, perhaps, McDonough learned that leading his men on and safely through difficult and dangerous missions involved confronting honestly his own fears of death or injury. The assorted characters in *Platoon Leader*—brave and cowardly, selfless and small-minded, inspiring and apathetic—make the psychological conflicts and resolutions in McDonough's account at least as absorbing as the graphic battle scenes."

—*Sea Power Magazine*

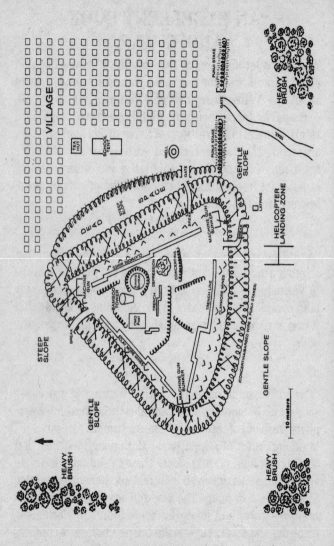

2d Platoon's Position aside the Village of Truong Lam, in Tam Quon District, Binh Dinh Province.

# PLATOON LEADER

## A Memoir of Command in Combat

# James R. McDonough

PRESIDIO

**BALLANTINE BOOKS • NEW YORK**

Books published by The Ballantine Publishing Group are available at quantity discounts on bulk purchases for premium, educational, fund-raising, and special sales use. For details, please call 1-800-733-3000.

A Presidio Press Book
Published by The Ballantine Publishing Group
Copyright © 1985 by James R. McDonough

www.ballantinebooks.com

ISBN 0-89141-800-8

Manufactured in the United States of America

First Mass Market Edition: February 2003

OPM  10  9  8  7  6  5  4  3  2  1

To those who served in our longest war. Though vilified and spurned by their countrymen, they honored their nation and themselves.

To Pat, Jim, Mike, and Matt. They made a better world than they found.

# CONTENTS

# PROLOGUE

Military men thrive on the telling of war stories. Contrary to the myth that men who have seen combat tend to keep it to themselves, I have found that we often talk too much about it. Forgive me, then, if this book appears to be another war story, for I make no claim to having experienced unique adventures in Vietnam. I feel now, as I felt then, that my own experience was relatively moderate. I am sure that many other units and many other men saw more action than did I or my platoon. If there were a contest to determine the number of hair-raising tales one could recount, I would hesitate to enter it. So many others have seen so much more.

Nor do I offer this book as the definitive description of the war in Vietnam. That would be impossible for anyone to do. The style of the war changed from year to year, from unit to unit, from place to place. There were no typical experiences. If anything was typical about the Vietnam experience, it was that it was different for everyone involved.

Since this book is neither an adventure yarn nor a definitive description of the war in Vietnam, one might ask, What is its purpose? In response I can only suggest that the book is about an American platoon leader in combat.

1

# CHAPTER 1

# AUGUST 1, 1971:
# LZ ENGLISH

Slowly the jeep pulls away, and I watch my driver, Phil Nail, trying hard to demonstrate his mastery over the alien vehicle. He has been driving only a few days, and his eyes dart nervously. His new job is a result of my final act of concern for the men of my former rifle platoon. Although Nail is uncomfortable, I am glad I had him transferred. As a rifleman, he was wounded three times. He's been lucky so far, but I know the odds are against his pulling through a fourth wounding. The longer he allows himself to stay in the relative safety of LZ English, the base camp for the 173d Airborne Brigade, the more likely that he will survive to the end of his stay in Vietnam. Having him transferred is the one small gesture I can make before going home, an act I hope will lessen, if only minutely, my feelings of guilt for going home on my feet. How well I know that there are many Phil Nails still out there in the bush. For them I can do nothing.

In the hot sun I stand beside the short airstrip of LZ English, waiting for the helicopter to take me to Camranh Bay, where the DC-10 waits to take me home. It is a quiet morning. From my vantage point on the small, leveled hill that houses the airstrip, I can see across the barbed wire fence to the rice paddies and the village of Bong Son beyond. Amid the tall, green rice, Vietnamese peasants are toiling away, here and there a domesticated water buffalo performing the timeless chores of Southeast Asian farming. Smoke wafts up from countless small homes and huts in the crowded village. The smells of Asia drift across the runway, intensified by the warmth of the sun and the stillness of the day. How quiet and serene it seems. Only the sandbagged wooden hut at the edge of the airstrip reminds me that a war is in progress.

I am not quite alone. A few yards to my right stands an army major in ill-fitting fatigues. His awkwardness of dress and his soft facial expression tell me at a glance that he has never been on the other side of the barbed wire, out in the field. In the wooden hut a soldier stands beside a field radio; nothing but static hums over the speaker. The soldier's rifle is the only weapon in sight.

I ignore them both. I want to be alone with my thoughts. Somehow I must rivet the picture of Bong Son and the countryside into my mind, and I feel I can only do it at this moment. Soon I will be gone, never to see it again. Before, I was too involved, too close to it, to remember it objectively. But now it is important for me to concentrate on these last few minutes on the ground in Binh Dinh province. Perhaps I am assuring myself that I have made it to the end. Perhaps I must convince myself that this is my last day with the 173d Airborne, and I am intact. That seemed a remote possibility when I began leading my platoon back in the early stages of my tour in Vietnam.

How long ago was that? Only a year? It seems I was much younger then, so much younger. And the men. Only a few are still around. Perhaps that was why Phil Nail was so smug when he shook my hand and said good-bye. So many of the others are gone. Even their replacements are gone, gone to early graves, hospital wards, shocked and horrified families, and years of questioning what happened, why it happened, and why it happened to them.

And how did I make it? Did I ask other men to do what I would not have done? Did I not take care of them? Was I too zealous in doing what was military? Did I contribute to the evil of this war in some callous, uncomprehending way? Or did I lessen that evil by doing what was right, by doing what had to be done, by doing what I was supposed to do?

My thoughts are interrupted. The major approaches me and asks me where I am going. I try to conceal my disdain for him, the disdain of a self-acclaimed veteran for the rear area soldier. It is an unfair disdain, but it is there, and he probably sees it.

"I'm going home," I tell him. He smiles, trying to share what he expects is my joy. I sense that, and my disdain grows. Doesn't he know that it's not joy? It's confusion; it's guilt; it's a sense of loss—but not joy. There is no room for joy in Vietnam.

"I'm a doctor," he tells me. "Psychiatrist, as a matter of fact." I wonder why he tells me that. I become wary. What is a psychiatrist doing here? He makes small talk, but I am only half-listening. Somewhere in his words he asks me my branch (infantry), and where I served in Vietnam. I point to what we call the Tiger Mountains, over in the north. "There," I say, "by the village of Truong Lam, not far from Tam Quon." He looks, but cannot see. He doesn't know the places; he doesn't know what comes with the names. The words mean nothing to him. I suppress my rage at this; many have died in the places that bear those names.

"What did you do?" he wants to know. I am wary again. Why is he asking these questions? The answers mean nothing to him. I speak in the past tense of the platoon I led. It has been a while since I led it (having been a staff officer in the last few months of my tour), and the men who were in it then are no longer there. The major picks up my mood; perhaps he is a good psychiatrist after all. "Do you ever dream about it?" he asks me.

I am surprised by the question. Dream about it? What does he mean? What is there to dream about? Is he testing a pet theory? Am I a subject of a research effort? "No, I don't dream about it," I tell him, with all the warmth with which I might say, "Shit on you, Bud!" He gets the message and backs off. I stand in silence waiting for the helicopter. The major is the final irony in a year filled with irony. Whoever sets in motion the forces that determine the life we lead has a tremendous flair for the ironic.

I marvel at the audacity of the question. My platoon was a part of my life, but I will not dream about it. I am determined I will not.

## January, 1974: Medford, Massachusetts

I wake from my sleep with a start. The sweat is damp and chilly on my chest; the sheets cling to me. I sit up, causing my wife to stir in the cool air. Outside the bedroom window I can see a gray morning forming beyond the barren trees that ring the backyard.

My heart is beating fast; my nerves feel frayed. The dream was vivid; I feel it lingering even now in the faint morning light. How many were there? Four? Five? No, there were more, and I knew them all. Who were they? Think, think! I knew them. I knew their names. Yes, that's it. They are West Point classmates of mine, all six of them graduates of the Military Academy, class of '69. Momentarily, their names escape me.

In the dream they moved so slowly, they talked so solemnly. And their eyes: big, wide, but nothing in them.

Glass eyes, looking at me with no expression. They were in full battle dress, each of them, bandoliers strapped across their chests, faces and hands camouflaged, their M-16s taped tightly to avoid metallic clangs. In single file—ranger file, as we called it—they came to me. We knelt in a muddy, barren hole in the ground, an enlarged foxhole or a fresh bomb crater. I'm not sure which. We talked, they and I, but I couldn't remember the words. We were discussing a mission; a map was spread on the ground in front of us, a map marred by mud and rain, barely legible in the dark jungle. When our discussion was over, they stood up to leave. How stiff they looked, how blank their stares.

Then I remembered some of the dialogue. "How are you doing?" I had asked them. I wanted to know. I felt as if I had to know. But no one answered. Slowly, again in ranger file, they walked off into the foliage, soundlessly fading into the background of my vision and my dream. By now I knew each of them. Their names, first and last, had come to me. Each one had come with me to Vietnam. Each one had died there.

I remembered the psychiatrist, and I cursed him in the quiet of the New England winter morning.

# CHAPTER 2

# THE ROAD TO WAR

The United States slid into Vietnam so gently, so slowly, it was all but imperceptible to the average observer. The early 1960s had bigger issues to contend with: a missile gap, a space race, a Cuban invasion, confrontation in Berlin, a nuclear face-off with the Soviet Union, an assassinated president, remote wars in faraway places of little importance to the United States, but seeming more important than the nonwars in Indochina.

In 1963 a boy coming of age in Brooklyn could identify more easily with the immediate issues of his own life than he could with Buddhist monks immolating themselves in grisly street scenes in Saigon. "Where is Saigon anyway?" he might ask while quickly thumbing through the newspaper to reach the box scores on the latest Yankee thriller against the Red Sox. Sports were important then. Politics were not. Girls were important, too, even if they were more incomprehensible than politics. World affairs are not the stuff of adolescence.

School was alleged to be important. All the adults said so. But in Brooklyn, school very often ended with graduation from high school, and that event was looming ever closer as 1963 passed into 1964. A time for decision was fast approaching. If not college, then what kind of work? And if college, then how to pay for it? And where to go?

The roads that lead young men to war are not political roads, or national and international roads, but individual roads. What propels young men (and, perhaps in the future, young women) to combat is not the draft. Those who are not destined for armed combat usually will not be drafted for armed combat. The pool of human resources is vast, and the number of riflemen is small. The person who wants to avoid the draft will avoid it. And in Vietnam, as the war went on, the numbers who successfully avoided the draft increased. So who fights? The fools, the uneducated, the knaves? I was none of these—or so I maintain. But I fought. What led me to it?

Certainly not the draft. Things were looking up in the winter of 1963–64 as I moved successfully through my senior year in high school. A New York State Regents Scholarship and a part-time evening job were answering the question of how to afford college. Although the thought of enlisting in what appeared to be a peacetime army was appealing to an eighteen-year-old yearning to break free of the nest, I was cautioned against running pell-mell into the ranks by my wise father, a veteran of World War II and twenty-two years of enlisted service. The advice made sense, and doubly so since there was a chance for an appointment to West Point. True, it was a remote chance in the highly politicized congressional districts of New York, but some exposure as a promising amateur boxer representing the American Legion gave me hope for a political appointment. At any rate, the army could wait; life was too exciting.

By the fall of 1964 Vietnam had become a bigger news item in the local papers. Still, it was too far away, and the United States too little involved, for it to be more than an item of passing interest to a young man planning his future in a world he already knew, a world alien in every way to Southeast Asia. Undergraduate study in civil engineering at Brooklyn Polytechnic allowed me to live at home and commute to college. It also allowed me to continue developing as a boxer in the nearby Brooklyn YMCA. I was expanding my intellectual horizons and feeding my hunger for adventure—right in my own backyard.

The summer of 1965 brought talk of sending American units to Vietnam. A year earlier the Gulf of Tonkin Resolution had laid the groundwork for the deployments, but the buildup was still not addressed as a war. It was not of much interest to a college student completing his first undergraduate year and embarking on an interesting summer surveying job in upstate New York.

A quirk of fate, however, brought the appointment to West Point. Nobody had qualified from the lower East Side of Manhattan. With a deft push of a pencil I was made an imaginary citizen of Manhattan. The phone call reached me at the surveying camp: "If you can get to West Point in three days, you can enter with the class of 1969. Want it?"

A moment of decision. Although young people are never properly prepared for these decisions, they must make them anyway: "I guess so." After all, I had told everybody I was seeking a nomination, and I had literally fought for it. I had taken the tests for it, and I had even been circumcised for it. Having given that much, it didn't seem right to turn it down.

I drove down to Staten Island that night. (My family had made the break from Brooklyn.) There was a big family party, a dinner out on the town, a proud ex-NCO father pounding his son the cadet-to-be on the back. I remember his face that night—the map of Ireland looking at me with sparkling blue eyes, pleased as punch that his boy was going to become one of "those goddamned officers."

Two days later I drove with my mother to her sister's home thirty miles from West Point. How different my mother's emotions were from my father's. As I left her to continue the last leg of the journey on my own, she became stricken with grief. She was saying good-bye to her boy, her sad dark eyes pouring out tears as she clutched at me with her small hands, her Italian features showing all the hurt a mother feels when she fears for what is about to happen to her son in his quest for his own life. It made me cry, and I was ashamed of it. How could I go to West Point, the school of military leaders, with tears in my eyes? That was a place for men, not mama's boys. Thank God, I had thirty miles for my eyes to unredden.

The first day of West Point was unbearable. Obviously everybody in the place, except for fellow unfortunates suffering their first day, was out to get me. But I made it to Taps and that night I resolved I would not quit. Not after all I had invested in that first day. I could not turn back now. Another resounding decision was made with the most groundless logic. But it was made, and I never wavered from it.

There were no two ways about it. West Point was a pain in the neck, literally: in the tradition of the times I braced my chin deep into my neck the entire first year. But West Point was exciting—from the very first days of "Beast Barracks" (the equivalent of basic training) there was talk of "the war in the jungles."

Summer training gave way to academics. Then, with painful slowness, we went back to summer training and more tactics. I easily equated the ruggedness of field life to the stark confrontations I had known in the boxing ring and the Brooklyn streets. It was a personal challenge, and I prided myself on my ability to cope with it. From the outset, I never imagined I would be any other than an infantry officer.

During the academic year of 1966–67, the war in Vietnam kept growing. There were weekly casualty reports; the battles were pitched. Graduates of the class of '66 were falling in battle.

This gave me pause for thought. It is one thing to hear of faraway battles. It is another to know people who have fought and died in them. Their deaths brought me face-to-face with finality in a way that reading statistics from other battles never could.

A trip away from West Point to the home of a graduated cadet killed in action was sobering. There was no joy in that household. My presence was awkward, a sad reminder that their son would never be back. I broke it off quickly. I could say nothing to help relieve the hurt they felt. I could only go away.

Nevertheless, I moved ever closer to the decision to become an infantry officer. I enjoyed leading men, and West Point gave me ample opportunity for that. And there were other things besides leadership. The schooling was good, and I did well. I continued boxing and sampled some other sports I had never even heard of in Brooklyn. The friendships were strong. The challenges were shared; the good times were many. I was proud of my classmates and cherished their respect. They could inspire me to try harder, and at the same time to enjoy a good laugh and not take myself too seriously. We were brothers bound by the intensity of our commitment to a common cause—graduation from West Point.

There were the girls—a few at first, and then in my last year, one very special girl. For the first time West Point became truly burdensome. The harassments of plebe year, the pressures of the academics, the regimentation of daily life, and the physical discomfort of tactical training all paled beside my impatience to graduate and be with the woman I loved. Would June 1969 ever come?

The war was becoming a reality. Back in 1966 and 1967 I believed it would end before my time came. I could pretend that the great drama of combat lay in my future, but in truth I knew that wars just did not last that long. Four years seemed to be the historical maximum for American wars, at least since the Revolutionary War. Yet the weekly casualty figures kept growing. The 173d Airborne Brigade suffered eight hundred casualties on Thanksgiving 1967, all of them in a single battalion. Tet of 1968 (January 31) saw the bloodiest fighting of the war to date. As Richard Nixon was inaugurated in January 1969, American dead totaled over four hundred weekly. West Point was compiling a lengthy and growing honor roll of those fallen in combat.

In February of 1969 I chose the infantry as my branch, and in March I volunteered for Vietnam. In April I wrote the commander of the 173d Airborne Brigade, whose unit was reputed to be the toughest regular army unit in Vietnam, and asked to serve in his outfit. On June 4 I graduated, and I was married at West Point four days later.

West Point had done its job well. The decisions to serve in the infantry, to join the only U.S. airborne brigade in the war, and to select Vietnam for my first full assignment were not decisions at all. They flowed with the same naturalness as falling in love. There may have been other options, but not for me: I had to serve my country, as I had to marry the woman I loved.

The road to war was now set, although there were to be a few stops along the way. The army, in its efficient way, allowed for a leave (honeymoon), a spate of schools (Airborne School, the Infantry Officers Basic Course, Jumpmaster School, Ranger School), and even a short stateside assignment to learn the basics of being a second lieutenant in front of soldiers. Fort Benning, Georgia, was not much of a setting for a new bride. In peacetime the Alabama-Georgia border might be considered quaint, but during a war, camps like Fort Benning assume a morbid assembly-line quality. People were just passing through, almost all of them on the way to war.

Airborne school was a unique experience. Although jumping out of airplanes in military formation was not without its thrills, running around getting ready for the jumps for two weeks in the hot August humidity was not the most enjoyable thing in the world. The twelve weeks of basic infantry schooling seemed beneath my dignity, as it did to all second lieutenants, but it did give me time to get to know my wife, if only between the hours of 7 P.M. and 5 A.M.

In September I learned that my wife was pregnant. I was excited, but before I could reflect on it we experienced our first separation. Ranger school began in November and ran through January. For fifty-six days I thought of nothing but survival. I learned I was not as tough as I pretended to be, but a lot tougher than I thought. After endless patrols through freezing Georgia mountains and frozen Florida swamps, unrelenting exposure to the elements, days and weeks with an hour or less sleep each night—snatched in bursts of five and ten minutes—starvation rations, and bone-breaking terrain, I actually looked forward to the relative comfort of Vietnam.

There was time, though, for a reunion with my now very pregnant wife; a move to Fort Bragg, North Carolina, and the 82d Airborne Division; and four very quick months that saw the birth of my son and two deployments with my rifle company. By June, the army was finished preparing me. I was ready to go into action.

I took some leave to show off my new son and to say my good-byes. I spent a few days with my parents, and then drove my wife and son to Virginia, where they would await my return. As I left my father we shook hands, and as I looked in his eyes I thought I saw a tear. How very different he looked from the proud father I saw the day I left for West Point. He looked overcome with fear. I had never seen my father cry. For the first time, I was afraid.

There was yet one more good-bye. My wife came with me to the plane that would take me from National Airport in Washington and start me on my way. Our two-month-old baby was with us.

"Don't worry," I said. "I'll make it back." The words sounded weak, but I wanted her to believe them. I wasn't sure I did.

In the next moment we kissed. Reluctantly I broke contact, forced myself to turn and walk away. I could not bring myself to look back even once at my wife and child. The pain was too great; my guilt at leaving them was too deep. Numbly I boarded the plane and found my seat. The army had spent a fortune getting me ready for whatever was ahead. I had no idea what to expect.

# CHAPTER 3

# WELCOME TO VIETNAM

The political world and my personal world had merged. Over two hundred of us winged across the Pacific in a chartered plane, as if we were off to a vacation in the Hawaiian Islands. Only our uniforms and the taut expressions on our faces gave us away.

I finished writing my first letter home and sealed it in the envelope I carried inside my shirt. I would mail it when we landed in Vietnam. It was the first of an unbroken string of letters I would write every day throughout the coming year, no matter where I might be (with the exception of the times I was physically incapacitated from wounds). I looked up at the pretty stewardesses. What a strange way to go to war.

I sat between two West Point classmates, good friends who had not only gone through the Academy with me, but who also had run the gauntlet of post-graduation army schools. Guy, sitting to my left, had lasted a bit longer than I, marrying a few months out of West Point, despite the objections of his wife's family about the uncertainty of marriage to a soldier going to war. On my right sat Barry, a carefree bachelor from Michigan, renowned for his good times and solid right hand. Barry and I had spent many a day sparring together, getting ready for the competition in our respective weight classes.

Both Guy and I were personally indebted to Barry.

One night in Panama, after completing the two-week jungle warfare course, Barry had saved Guy and me, both newly married, some embarrassment by going off with three ladies of the night who had approached us as we sat in a Panama City bar. The ladies were enriched, Barry was left with a great story, and Guy and I were spared the awkwardness of explaining ourselves to the ladies that night or to our wives later.

It was reassuring to enter the war zone in the company of close friends. Guy would be among the first of the class of '69 to die in Vietnam. Barry made it to his seventh month when he was caught unarmed at Fire Base Mary Ann along with seventy-six other Americans who had their weapons locked up for safekeeping when they came in from the field. A fighter to the end, Barry was found with his hands gripped around the throat of a dead Viet Cong whose face was battered by Barry's punches. As for Barry, he had a bullet in his head, a testament to the unfairness of the match.

These events still lay in our future, however, as the big DC-10 eased itself into a nighttime landing at Bien Hoa. The entire planeload strained to look down at the approaching ground. Very little was visible outside the glass portals save the lights of the runway and the occasional outline of distant terrain as it cut against the shadowy skyline. We all braced as the wheels touched the ground, as if trying, in that instant, to absorb the shocks of the year to come. The faces of the young soldiers on their first tour were awed, confused, full of wonder and fear. The faces of the veterans on their second and third tours were knowing, but just as afraid. The latter waited for the shock of incoming rounds that might catch us like so many targets encased in the lumbering plane. How incongruous it was to sit there amidst upholstered splendor, expecting to go into battle. It was the first of the war's many ironies.

In the black beyond the lights of the plane, out in the darkness that our eyes could not penetrate from within our brilliant cocoon of artificial light and air-conditioned comfort, was Vietnam—the foreboding place that had grown in our minds from an obscure, unfamiliar place-name of little consequence in our personal lives, to a destiny that promised fear, discomfort, danger, and possibly death. We began to sweat even before the big engines turned down.

Slowly, a heavy-set sergeant grunted aboard the plane and, in the weighty tones of a man bored by the monotony of his job and weary from the lateness of the hour, announced to his attentive audience that they had arrived in Vietnam.

We were hardly astounded by the news, but our attention remained fixed as he described, without the slightest inflection, the procedures we were to follow should we come under mortar attack. At last we were hearing something that lived up to our expectations of arriving in a war-torn area. Nevertheless, our briefer did not seem overly concerned, and it was our general suspicion that he had never, nor could he ever, run off the airstrip to get away from incoming rounds. It was doubtful that he was even awake. His speech droned on. The plane got hotter. In Vietnam, as in all other wars, the army had perfected the technique of "hurry up and wait." The sergeant finished with an uninspiring "Stay alert! Stay alive!" At any rate, the speech was over and we could go.

We disembarked slowly from the sanitized cylinder that had picked us up in the world we knew and deposited us in this strange land. It was a humid night, dark and foreboding, a night punctuated by the roar of jet engines as they moved to their positions along the runway. In the yellow light of the terminal we could see for the first time the nature of the American character in

Vietnam. Strained-looking men loitered everywhere: American soldiers getting ready to depart, some on leave (rest and recuperation, or R and R), but most going home. These were men who knew well the madness of Vietnam, men with stark looks in their eyes, set mouths, and faces that seemed aged beyond their years. What they were thinking I could not fathom, but they looked upon the new arrivals with great disdain and, it was plain to see, little pity. The artificial light, the humid stench, the inhospitable glances of the veterans, combined to increase the gloom of our arrival. What could it be like beyond?

The processing, like many things in the army, was mindless drudgery: fill out a form, secure your valuables, open your bags, move on in line, exchange your money. After two hours we filed into screened buses, regular military vehicles with wire nets over the windows to deflect grenades tossed at us as we drove along the darkened road. Still, no weapons were issued to us.

We arrived at the 90th Replacement Detachment, the holding unit for so many Vietnam arrivals during the war years, found bunks and went off into fitful sleep. We spent two days processing our records, glancing at the sights of Vietnam beyond our containment area, awaiting orders for unit assignments, and wondering what fate awaited us.

In the coming year we would learn how little our decisions determined our futures. Destiny is not born of decision; it is born of uncontrollable circumstances. Throughout the year to come, this point would be driven home time and time again. Rational decision making or technical and physical skills may save you once or twice. But a man in combat is exposed a thousand times. A gust of wind blows at the right moment to take the mortar round ten yards farther to explode harmlessly behind you. A tree grows for fifty years only

to absorb the grenade fragment that would otherwise
have entered your heart. A blade of grass, a bent
branch, or an article of equipment deflects a speeding
bullet enough to send it harmlessly through your flop-
ping shirt or boneless flesh—or savagely through your
brain or liver. And as you move mindlessly through the
replacement system, the whim of an unseen clerk sends
you to a unit in a quiet sector—or to a unit that will
take its men like lambs to the slaughter.

And so we waited, not yet knowing much about the
hands of fate. We filled our time with light banter, some
of us friends of many years, others friends of a few days.
We talked of our pasts, our homes. We traded stories we
had heard about Vietnam. We wondered, but did not
speak of, what was in store for us.

We watched the beautiful mornings of Vietnam
take form, the brilliant sun rising into the crisp, blue
sky, reflecting on the rich green of the foliage below. We
watched the delicate women in their captivating long,
high-slit dresses worn over graceful, satiny pants. They
looked elegant, softly sensuous, as they walked to work
on tiny high-heeled shoes. We saw few Vietnamese men,
and those we did see were old, hard-looking little men,
the ubiquitous cigarette dangling from their craggy
mouths, smoke curling up past dark, knowing eyes. I
wondered how we looked to them. Their blank expressions told us little.

So we kept to ourselves and waited. One by one the
orders came in, and each hour our numbers were fewer.
Already more new arrivals were coming in behind us.
We tried to appear like veterans to them, but our own
wide-eyed eagerness betrayed us. Guy and Barry soon
left me, each going his own way. The conversations continued, growing increasingly stale.

At last my orders came, deluding me into thinking
for an instant that I might be in control of my destiny

after all. I was going to the 173d Airborne Brigade, the unit I had solicited in my last year at West Point. It was the first American army unit to deploy to Vietnam, the descendant unit of the 503d Airborne Infantry Regiment that had jumped into the Philippines in World War II. For years, it had been the strategic reserve of the American forces in Vietnam, the "fire brigade" that went to where the action was fiercest. It was a unit in which I would draw an extra $110 a month for serving with a paratrooper outfit. It was a proud unit with a reputation of being proven in combat. The fact that it was now fulfilling a "pacification mission" gave me some pause. This didn't sound very warlike. Perhaps I would not see any action in Vietnam after all.

From the replacement camp at Bien Hoa I moved north toward the 173d. Of the more than two hundred who had arrived together, only a handful of us went up to Phu Tai, the rear support base of the 173d. There we were processed into the brigade before moving up to the forward battalions stationed forty miles to the north at the town of Bong Son, a Viet Cong stronghold in Binh Dinh province.

We flew into Qui Nhon, the nearby U.S. Air Force Base and the site of the medical facility that cared for the wounded and sick U.S. and allied casualties of Vietnam's central coastal area. Qui Nhon was a transportation center, a supply depot where people and equipment moved farther into the war or farther away from it. The war did not seem close there. It seemed a civilized place. One could just sense that somewhere inside those massive buildings were flush toilets.

Nonetheless, a growing curiosity about war lingered in the back of my mind. What was it like? What was I getting into? If only someone could have told me and revealed the secrets, instead of just hinting.

As I stood in an oversized airplane hangar that

straddled the runway, my eyes searched the crowd, looking for someone who might know. The brilliant Vietnamese sun was defused through the high, broad windows of the hangar and reflected off the rusting metallic walls, giving the busy atmosphere a greenish glow. Every which way, men in fatigues and worn boots hurried about their business. The thick smell of grease belched from a hastily erected grill offering American-style hamburgers to airfield workers and transient passengers, the sizzling noises lost amid the roar of engines on the airstrip outside.

My eyes picked out a gaunt figure leaning against a beam supporting the hangar structure. His grubby fatigues sported a darkened lieutenant's bar, and on his left and right shoulders I saw the unit patch of the 173d Airborne Brigade, an oversized bayonet floating on a feathered wing of what must have belonged to a massive bird. According to army tradition a soldier wears the patch of the unit he is assigned to on his left shoulder, and the unit patch of the outfit with which he has served in combat on the right shoulder. This man's uniform told me that he was a first lieutenant currently assigned to the 173d Airborne Brigade and that he had already been in combat with them. Wearing the same unit patch only on my left sleeve advertised, to my chagrin, that I was still green. I made my way to the lieutenant.

As I approached and the crowd between the two of us thinned, I could see his sunken eyes. Two black, glazed pupils stared out at me in an expression of mute horror. Although the man rested against the beam, his manner was far from relaxed. His neck was taut to the point of creating a noticeable vibration that coursed downward through his body. His boots had long lost their original blackness, showing instead the whitened stains of leather too often wet and too often dried. The tops had begun to crack away from the heavily worn soles. In his hand he carried a small gym bag that could have held little more than a smattering of clothing.

"Pardon me, lieutenant. I'm Lt. Jim McDonough," I said, trying not to sound too eager.

He looked at me and said nothing. I went on: "I'm on my way up to join 'the Herd.' " I used the nickname of the 173d, trying to sound authoritative.

I interpreted his silence as the maturity of the hardened combat veteran responding to the newcomer. It would have intensified my self-consciousness if I hadn't been distracted by the stink that came from the man. He smelled of heavy sweat that had seeped from his pores and dried many times over a long period of time. But the smell was more than a body odor; it was a smell of death: strong, pungent, and repulsive.

"Look, I don't mean to intrude, but I was wondering if you could tell me a little about the 173d," I said.

As my words registered he sprang away from the beam and stood close to me, staring into my face. His smell, his look of horror, and his tension startled me. As his face contorted into speech, I realized that madness, not maturity, marked the man.

His lips twisted into a grimace and the gleeful evil in his eyes rocked my senses. "It's wonderful," he said. "Nothing like it in the world. You'll get more than your share of killing. The bodies are everywhere, and in no time at all you'll have a collection of ears that will make those rear echelon mother fuckers green with envy."

I could not believe it. He went on, but I lost track of what he was saying. He was practically drooling, as if savoring every recollection of the carnage he was describing. Could he be putting me on? Could this be a mean trick? I wasn't self-conscious anymore. I wanted to hit him.

But he wasn't toying with me. The man was serious.

He was caught up in the emotion of the scenes he was describing.

". . . and then I strung the body up in the tree. The men said, 'Stop!' but I wanted them to see that stiff swinging in the helicopter downdraft as we extracted. I showed them what I thought of those gooks." He was no longer looking at me. His eyes were fixed on the crazed, garbled scenes in his mind. His neck muscles tensed yet some more; his arms moved in jerky gestures, the ridiculous gym bag dangling from his fingers.

". . . maggots had already eaten at his bloody stump. I stepped on them and mashed them into his rotting corpse. Goddamned dink!"

I backed away from him, slowly at first, then quickly when I saw that he didn't even notice my leaving. He continued talking to himself, his arms flapping in the musky air of the hangar. I fled in horror.

Earlier, I had been afraid only of being physically maimed or killed. But now I saw that there was another threat, that of a madness born of terror and dehumanizing ferocity. The veteran lieutenant was mad. Perhaps once he had been like me. He was alive, but he had not really survived. Physically he was unmarked; spiritually he was dead; mentally he was as mutilated and twisted as the most grotesque cadaver he had described. If this could happen to him, could it happen to me? I was shaken to my bones.

I later learned that only a few hours before I met him, shortly before dawn of that same day, the lieutenant had lain in ambush with a "Hunter-Killer" team (a reconnaissance/combat element of six men) beside a trail while two battalions of North Vietnamese walked by hurriedly. Twenty claymore mines, each with seven hundred steel miniballs compressed into C-4 blasting powder (a charge more powerful than TNT), dotted the trail from which their electrical wires fed back to the lieutenant's arms, where in a makeshift apparatus of two hinged boards he had placed their respective generators. At the moment of decision he compressed the boards, blowing the mines and devastating the enemy column. Before the smoke cleared, the lieutenant entered the kill zone, pumping round after round into the dead and dying enemy. Under his frenzied onslaught and the initially reluctant but then desperately rapid fire of the small American element, the enemy broke and ran.

The trail was littered with twenty-two North Vietnamese bodies, a gruesome testament to the military efficiency of the lieutenant. But during the moment of his decision to initiate the combat, his mind had cracked. As he executed his violent assault through the shattered column of the dazed enemy, he was a man no more. By the time his commander arrived, a short while later, it was clear that the lieutenant had to go. The blood dripping from his hands had drained his senses. His own men shrank in horror at his bloodlust. I saw the site of the ambush a few days later and heard the story of his frenzied attack. As I stood amidst the stench of the decomposing bodies I understood what had happened. I could feel sorry for the lieutenant then, but there in the airport at the moment of our meeting I knew only revulsion from the horror of his morbid glee.

I was still shaken as I loaded my few personal belongings into the back of a three-quarter-ton truck. A few other soldiers joined me. The disparity in our ranks meant nothing as we sat amidst the pile of duffle bags and extraneous supplies accompanying us to the Brigade's rear area camp at Phu Tai. As we left the gate at Qui Nhon I looked back in the direction of the lieutenant. He was standing where I left him, his eyes still fixed on the grotesque scenes in his mind.

I forced myself to look away, trying to concentrate

on something else. I looked at my fellow travelers—
mostly young innocents like me but here and there a
hardened face telling of time already spent in Vietnam.
I glanced out the back of our uncovered truck. The sides
of the road were an unbroken mosaic of rusting soda
and beer cans and browned paper wrappings, a graphic
symbol of the degree to which American commercialism
had poured into the Vietnamese economy. We had
brought our throw-away society with us to the crowded
coastal lowlands, and here it lay at the edge of another
culture.

As we slowed in our passage through a crowded village, I noted the densely populated pockets of civiliza-
tion scattered along the road. Dusty houses and dusty
people pressed right up to the highway, which was
really only a small street that barely allowed the passage
of two medium-size vehicles coming from opposite directions. Smiling children waved happily at us as we
passed by, their smooth oval faces alive with grinning
teeth and sparkling eyes. I brightened. They looked
warm, glad to see us. I extended my arm to wave at a
group of boys standing dangerously close to our passing
truck. One grabbed my sleeve, then another, my arm.
Running along beside us, they tore at my wristwatch. I
tried to pull back but too many hands were tearing at
my hand, my arm, my shirt. Fingernails dug into my
wrist under the watchband. With my free arm I clutched
at the side of the truck, fighting desperately to keep
from falling into the growing throng of children. Several
soldiers clutched at me to keep me aboard. At last, the
watch broke free and the children relinquished their
hold. I lurched back into the bed of the truck.

"Better not wave any more, lieutenant," one of the
hard faces said. I knew I had a lot to learn about Vietnam.

On the afternoon of the next day I made the next
forty-mile journey, by helicopter this time, to the Brigade's

headquarters, LZ English, only three miles south of my designated battalion at LZ North English, the home of the 4th Battalion, 503d Infantry (Airborne), one of the four infantry battalions of the 173d Airborne Brigade. By late afternoon I pulled into LZ North English, having covered the distance by jeep. There was only one leg of the journey left, the quick helicopter ride to the platoon I would lead, at the last frontier in the midst of the enemy. But before that, I had one final day in relative security.

I drew my weapons, wrote a quick letter home, and dropped off my few remaining personnel records (the rest had been left at Phu Tai). At the company rear headquarters at LZ North English I could hear the tactical radio reports of casualties coming in. There was a great deal of noise everywhere—helicopters flying in and out, artillery rounds exploding out of their tubes— all of it in support of lonely American units out beyond the barbed wire, too far away to be seen. Tomorrow I would be out there. I was bracing myself.

The battalion commander met me in the evening. He was an uncertain-looking man who had been visibly wearied by the war—hardly the image of the fighting leader I had been groomed to expect. He asked me if my papers were in order and if I had a will. He wanted to impress me with the seriousness of the situation I was in. He succeeded!

The following morning I was taken by helicopter to the site of the ambush led by the lieutenant I had met in Qui Nhon. The commander wanted to expose me to one more experience before allowing me to take over my platoon. He gave me a description of the successful ambush. The twenty-two bodies still lay on the trail, and dried blood streaks led off into the bushes. Here I learned to identify a smell that I would come to know well during my tour in Vietnam. It was the smell of death, a unique and repulsive smell that seemed to cover me like a stinking blanket. Later, it would seem that the smell came even before the death, as if it were a precursor of the dying that was to follow. The stench seemed to gather as a warning. The dying would then be inevitable; it had to come to account for the smell. There was no rational explanation for it. I learned not to question it, only to acknowledge its warning and to prepare myself for the eventuality.

"Seen enough, lieutenant?" the commander asked.

"Yes, sir," I replied.

Late in the afternoon I made the final part of my journey to combat. Loaded down with the gear I would need to sustain me in the field, I walked the few meters to the helipad. The clouds of dust billowing up at my feet obscured the uncertainty of my steps. The sun was setting low in the sky. For five years I had been readied for combat; now I would face it.

# CHAPTER 4

# 2D PLATOON

The Huey helicopter descended upon a barren circle of earth. The green of the heavy undergrowth along the perimeter of the landing zones melded into the rich brown earth, so stark against the verdant background that it seemed almost red. The *whump-whump-whump* of the helicopter blades created a wind that tore at the tattered clothing of the soldiers securing the landing zone. Three men were posted on the edge of the clearing, a fourth guided the chopper in. These were soldiers of my platoon: 2d Platoon, Bravo Company, 4th Battalion, 503d Infantry (Airborne). A normal platoon-size element of a rifle company calls for forty-three men. On that day, there were twenty-two present for duty.

I alighted from the helicopter, which hesitated only long enough to kick off some supplies and a canvas mail sack. That sack, I would later realize, was the one link with the world left behind. Beneath its drawn strings were the messages reminding us of a saner world totally divorced from our daily existence.

As I ducked under the treacherous blades of the straining helicopter, I approached the infantryman who had guided us in, yelling in his ear above the din for the location of the platoon leader. He jerked his thumb over his shoulder, throwing me a look of utter contempt as the ascending helicopter fouled my clean uniform with clouds of dust. The security element withdrew from its

position and retreated to the barbed wire that encircled
the lone infantry platoon that guarded this remote corner of the world. Making a mental note of the apparent
disrespect from the first soldier of my platoon I had en-
countered, I followed the infantrymen through the
twisting break in the wire into the platoon position.

By 1970 the United States had witnessed the bank-
ruptcy of the strategic hamlet program in Vietnam, but
was slow in discontinuing its tactical implementation.
This was the plan whereby the dependency of the Viet
Cong guerrillas upon the peasantry of the countryside
was to be severed. Through government control of the
local civilians, the enemy was to be left without the lo-
gistical base, the recruiting pool, and the moral support
needed to sustain themselves in combat. It was a theory
the British had adapted to Vietnam after their experience with it in Malaysia. Like many theories applied in
Vietnam, it was poor in practice.

The enemy was of the people here in Binh Dinh
province. They were, in every respect, indistinguishable
from the peasantry. There was no way to separate the
two. The village people were their family. All the barbed
wire, all the curfews, all the military presence in the
world, could not sever the ties between them. Even
when enemy supplies dried up from among the local
population, they were forthcoming from North Vietnam. This was not Malaysia. This was more than a civil
war. It was an insurrection supported by invasion, fu-
eled and fanned by total commitment from an external
nation. Much had been invested in the strategic hamlet
program in the 1960s, but by the end of the decade only
the most artificial data (and there was plenty of that in
Vietnam—briefed daily up and down the military and
civilian hierarchies) could qualify it as a success.

Nevertheless, acceptance of reality is slow in any bureaucracy. It is excessively so in the military. Accordingly,

in the summer of 1970, 2d Platoon, Bravo Company, working apart from its parent company, was given the pacification mission of securing the village of Truong Lam in Tam Quon district, Binh Dinh province. Of all the locales in Vietnam, perhaps none was known to be more Viet Cong–controlled than this one.

Located seven kilometers east of the north-south Highway 1 (the major and, for much of its length, the only paved road in Vietnam) and three kilometers west of the South China Sea, the village of Truong Lam's population was approximately thirteen hundred old men, women, and young children. The adult, and even the teenage, males were all absent, fighting their endless war (they did not have a year's rotation as the Americans did) either as Viet Cong or as soldiers in the Army of the Republic of Vietnam (ARVN).

Life was hard for either group. The ARVNs (pronounced *Arvins*), by and large, never got home. Those who did ran the risk of being matriculated into the North Vietnamese–instituted "reeducation camps" in 1975. The Viet Cong generally stayed in the area, but their casualty rates were exceedingly high, and for them wounds were often fatal.

Into the midst of this war-torn land were inserted twenty-two able-bodied American soldiers and a platoon leader. As I made my way to the platoon command post (CP) the sun had already dropped from the sky. Night in the tropics comes fast, and even as I approached the outgoing platoon leader, the shadows had begun to obscure his facial features. I found him lying on his stomach in a depression, situated roughly in the center of the platoon. As I bent over to introduce myself, he motioned for me to get down. Assuming that perhaps I was dangerously exposed, I lay down next to him.

"Hello, I'm Jim McDonough," I said, feeling some-

what awkward being so formal while lying on my
stomach.

"Tom Rolfe," he said. "Are you here to take my
place?" He was unable to conceal eagerness.

"Yes," I replied. "Can you tell me what's going on
here?"

As he began briefing me, it became apparent that
the platoon was not the object of his thoughts. I asked
questions about the dispositions of the squads, the per-
sonalities of the men, the tactics of the enemy, the attitude of the villagers. He responded by telling me about
how difficult the job was, how much his family needed
him, how he had never asked to be an infantry lieutenant, how dangerous and uncomfortable his life had
been of late, and how he did not deserve to be wounded
or killed. He was overcome by the fear that on this last
night in the field, the enemy would somehow snatch
survival away from him.

As the hours passed and we did not move from our
position in the midst of the platoon, I became acutely
conscious of our protected posture. All about us I could
hear movement. I saw the silhouettes of soldiers as they
moved about, setting up their positions for the night. I
noted that at least one patrol departed from the perimeter, but that the orders for the patrol did not come from
the lieutenant. Rolfe lay there chattering aimlessly into
the night, describing again and again for me the wife
and two children he had left behind. Gradually, he
honed in on his point.

"You've got to understand, I did this for them.
They need me. They need me in one piece."

Nervous silence followed as I tried to find his eyes in
the darkness. What was he talking about? The question
arose even as the answer was forming all around me.

"They know what to do. They're good soldiers."
Silence again. He was shocked by his own confession,

but at the same time he was urged on by the baring of his soul.

"I could have been a hero. Sometimes I even wanted to be. But I had to think of my family. You see, don't you? Most of these men don't have any family. They're just boys."

The shamefulness of his words hit me like a club. He was not the leader of this platoon. He felt no responsibility for the mission; he felt no compassion for the men. In his mind, the other members of the platoon existed for only one reason: to protect him, to keep him alive. The men were expendable; he was not. He had reason to live; they did not.

I wanted to crawl away, but it was dark and I had no idea where to go. We stopped talking. I had nothing more to ask. He wanted to say no more about his personal concerns. He knew he had gone too far, but he didn't care. His only concern in the world was to leave that knoll as soon as possible. The platoon and I could be damned. If he survived, justice would have been done. That night nothing else mattered for him. His soul lay naked, stripped of pride, guilt, and shame. They were affectations of the civilized world. Out here, only living mattered.

Unable to sleep, unable to move, I lay there wondering which I would turn out to be: the crazed killer I had met in Qui Nhon or the blatant coward beside me in the dark. Which one was more devoid of humanity, I did not know.

Later, after almost three months in the field, I saw Rolfe again. As the battalion adjutant, secure behind the battalion perimeter of LZ North English, he had adopted an air of bravado. In the safety of the officers' club, he told me of his brave deeds. He talked as one who had seen it all. In his own words he became the dashing, fearless leader of combat infantrymen. He even had a few combat awards for valor, the procurement of which fell among his duties as battalion adjutant. But the most amazing thing of all was his belief in every one of his own words. As far as he consciously knew, he was all he claimed to be. He had forgotten how he lay quivering in the dark, praying the enemy would not come.

From that point on I began to watch myself carefully. Was I really what I thought I was? Or had I deluded myself as effectively as Rolfe had?

In the morning the helicopter came to take Rolfe away. He brought himself to his knees, which was as high as I had seen him rise since my arrival the night before and, without a word of farewell to me or any of the soldiers, made a desperate dash to the helicopter. In an instant he was gone, and I recognized with a feeling of awe that I was now in command. It was time to survey my domain.

Second Platoon's command post was a little knoll rising barely twenty feet above the village of Truong Lam. Here a triangular-shaped position, twenty-five meters to a side, overlooked the crowded village barely twenty meters away. The village itself was an inverted L-shape, its east-west leg lying across the northern flank of 2d Platoon and its north-south leg lying due east of the command post.

This configuration placed the platoon above the village but practically on the interior corner of the L. Between Truong Lam and the surrounding countryside lay a double row of concertina barbed wire, coiled wire with razor-edged protrusions all along its length. In the midst of the concertina was upright regular barbed wire with lengths of more barbed wire angling up from the ground through the concertina rolls, ultimately attached to the upright barbed wire. This maze of wire, despite all its hooks and barbs, could be penetrated in approximately forty-five minutes by an experienced enemy sapper who would slip through it unclothed. In recognition of this, trip flares and mines had been laced into the wire. Additionally, the Vietnamese equivalent of the national guard, the Regional Forces (RF), disparagingly known as "rough puffs," inhabited the interior of the village in platoon-size strength. The virtue of this force, I was soon to discover, was mixed, but its officer leadership was unquestionably bad.

Around 2d Platoon's position was another maze of barbed wire, the only difference in it being that about six more rolls of concertina were piled fore and aft of the perimeter. Amidst the wire were bamboo "punji" stakes, bamboo poles honed to a fine point, hardened by fire, and embedded in the ground. Trip flares laced this jungle of wire and bamboo, and behind the last roll of wire were fifty-four claymore mines, a devastating charge of dynamite-like C-4 explosives with steel ball bearings packed into their hardened paste like so many metallic peas in a convex of frozen mashed potatoes. These mines were electronically detonated by hand-held generators (called "clackers") that fed wire into the mine itself. The clackers lined the wall of the four-foot trench running all along the inside of the perimeter. It was here that the men would fight. All along the trench were placed extra ammunition, flares, light antitank weapons (LAWs), fragmentation grenades, and flak jackets (antishrapnel protective vests). Each squad would defend a leg of the triangle, provided all three squads were inside the wire when the fighting began, which was unlikely since one squad was usually out on patrol at any given time. Therefore, three strong points were situated so that each could control the approaches to the other two with its M-60 machine gun, a fierce weapon that was the mainstay of small unit automatic fire.

The command position was located, in classical fashion, dead center in the middle of the platoon where a shallow foxhole, slightly reminiscent of a grave, had been hollowed out. The pièce de résistance of this fragile citadel, right out of a good French Foreign Legion yarn, was a bamboo tower rising forty feet into the air. God knows what the original plan had been for the tower, when it was built years ago by the Vietnamese unit that occupied this ground. But its platform had been reinforced with sandbags, and at great risk an observer could serve as a lookout. (In spite of myself, I would use it before my stay in this spot was over.)

There were three breaks in the wire to allow for entrance and egress to and from the platoon position. The landing zone for helicopters, our supply line and only link with supporting headquarters, was outside the wire to the south. Beyond that, the land sloped off into dry crop land intermingled with heavy undergrowth. To the north, rice paddies covered thousands of square meters, interspaced with dry areas of lush vegetation, excellent positions for the enemy to lie in ambush. To the west, toward Highway 1, were intermittent high ground and more rice paddies. Here the terrain was most hostile. The enemy could use it for a number of vantage points to observe and bring fire on my platoon position. Within fifty meters of the wire, the cover was good, and I immediately recognized it for what it was: enemy territory. The east was dominated by the village, and immediately beyond that were sand dunes leading to the South China Sea, just out of sight over a slight rise.

The nearest friendly unit was my company command post, about three kilometers away, consisting of the headquarters, one platoon, and three 81-millimeter mortars. The company, I came to learn, was led by a very nonaggressive company commander who rarely ventured outside of his CP, which left the intervening territory to my responsibility. Another American unit lay four thousand meters to my west, but for all the enemy between us and it, it could have been four thousand miles. To the south about five thousand meters were a number of Vietnamese units. Months later I would see how effective they were as I led a relief force into one of their positions, which had been completely overrun, all of their fifty men killed.

In this lonely environment, as the sole officer in charge of an area covering some twenty square kilometers, I began my combat tour. It was here, after all the years of preparation, that I would really learn the rudiments of military leadership. But as I began to grasp my situation that tropical morning of my first day in command of a platoon of infantry in the midst of the Vietnam war, I wondered what I should do.

# CHAPTER 5

# TAKING CHARGE

I was alone. That was my first sensation as a leader. The men were going about the morning's business—breaking out C rations, relieving themselves, shaving, brushing their teeth. They moved among each other comfortably, a word here, a smile there. I could hear snatches of conversation: "A good night's sleep . . ." "Only ninety days left." Occasionally a man would nod in my direction, or glance at me for a fleeting moment.

I gathered up my belongings—weapon, web gear, and rucksack—and moved toward the command post. I needed a few minutes to gather my thoughts before I made my debut as platoon leader. I knew it was going to be a tricky business.

I had assumed that I would have a company commander nearby to give me my orders. But I had not even met him yet; I would not meet him for weeks. The fact was, I was totally on my own. What should I do? Whose advice could I ask? The platoon sergeant's? The squad leaders'? In time I would listen to their ideas and incorporate them with my own, but I could hardly begin my tour with "Well, what do you think we ought to do, men?" No, I knew that the basic decisions were mine to make.

The first few moments would be crucial. Obviously I was the object of interest that morning. Everyone was wondering what the new lieutenant would be like, and

I would be telling them with my first words, my gestures, my demeanor, my eyes. I would have no grace period in which to learn my way around. This was a life and death environment. If I began with a blunder, my credibility as a leader would be shot, and so might some of the men.

I decided to begin by giving my attention to tactics. In a military environment, everything is determined by tactical considerations. Where you sleep, when you sleep, where you go, what you do, and in whose company you do it—all are dictated by underlying tactical necessities. I would communicate my style of leadership through my tactical instructions.

As I surveyed the soldiers, the nearby village, the distant rice paddies, the heavy undergrowth, the varied terrain, my mind raced back over the years of tactical training I had received. Conscious of the stares of the men, I hoped to appear composed as I fought back the panic of having to decide both quickly and correctly.

The first thing that occurred to me was the necessity of sending out patrols. Our mission in Vietnam was to control the countryside, but we could hardly do that if we stayed within the relative security of the platoon position. If our actions were strictly defensive, the enemy would be free to pick their tactics. The initiative would be theirs, and this would eventually disprove the illusion of security that the perimeter wire offered. My training told me that a completely defensive unit is a prime target for an overwhelming attack. I decided to send out three squad-size patrols a day, each at a different time, leaving two squads within the perimeter at any given moment. One squad would therefore be ready to react immediately to any action initiated by the patrolling squad, while the third squad would defend the platoon position. The trick would be to vary the timing, route, and specific mission of each patrol. While reconnaissance would be the order of the daytime patrols, they could swiftly convert to combat if the enemy was sighted. Moreover, they would attest to the United States presence in the countryside, and (so I thought at the time) a Vietnamese government presence as well.

Night patrols would be essential to complete the disruption of the enemy. Their orders would be to set up ambushes; their purpose was not to reconnoiter the enemy but to kill him as he walked into the "kill zone" (the ambushers' prime area of fire).

The enemy seemed to own the night. They laid down the mines and knew where they were located. Patrols were risky enough in the daytime, but there was a chance that we could sight a clue to a booby trap location. At night, it was pure luck. Either you stepped on one or you didn't.

The enemy also had a great deal of assistance in picking up the movement of the American patrols, often turning the ambushers into the ambushed. The villagers might pick up our noises as we exited the wire. If they were hostile to us, a certain candle or a radio switched on or off might signal our initial direction. If we were pinpointed, the odds would be very much against us. Nothing is more vulnerable to aggressive attack than a squad lying in ambush once it has been flanked. Without the element of surprise 90 percent of the combat advantage is lost as well. Stealth, long routes, doubling back, frequent shifting of ambush sites, and other ruses might decrease the possibility of pinpoint detection, but they increased the chances of hitting a booby trap or walking through an enemy ambush position. Although I knew it would be risky, it was imperative that we patrol at night. Therefore, I resolved, we would.

And where should I put myself in overseeing the operation of the platoon? In combat leadership, as in real estate, location is everything. I was the platoon leader, and the patrolling would be done by squad-size elements. Normally there were ten men in a squad, and four squads in a rifle platoon (one of them a weapons squad, the other three rifle squads), but personnel strengths being what they were, my squads were down to only six or seven men apiece, and there were only three squads. I would be risking oversupervision of the patrolling squad (whose direction was better left to the squad leader) if I went with it. I would also be away from the majority of my platoon back at the perimeter. On the other hand, to stay with the two squads in the perimeter would deny me the knowledge of the terrain in which my platoon operated and the opportunity to evaluate the quality of the patrols, the major offensive activity of my tactical position. Moreover, I would not be sharing in the highest-risk operations of my men and therefore might lose their respect. I might also miss my best chance to appreciate their perceptions, needs, and attitudes. Finally, I might slip into a defensive attitude myself, and that attitude would eventually overtake the entire platoon.

I resolved my dilemma with a compromise. I would go out with every other patrol until I had established my leadership. After that I would rotate my patrolling so that I joined one squad in every twenty-four-hour period. In that way I would be in the perimeter roughly two thirds of the time, yet I would avoid all the disadvantages of not going on patrol at all.

When I was on patrol, the squad leader would be in charge as long as he handled the situation effectively. I would exercise my prerogatives only in an emergency, or if we were joined by another squad from the platoon. In essence, I would not act as the squad leader, but would coordinate the actions of the entire platoon once contact was made (the proper role for the platoon leader).

If a patrol made contact with the enemy and it lasted for any length of time, a second squad would be sent to react. If I were inside the perimeter at such a time, I would move out with the reaction squad. I firmly believed it was the duty of the combat leader to "move to the sound of the guns," especially when the majority of the unit was engaged.

All my thoughts were reviewed and the basic decisions made in the time it took me to move to the command post and settle my gear in place—not more than fifteen minutes. Again and again during the coming months I would refine the details, but the essence of the decisions remained firm. I was not, however, brimming with the self-confidence such abrupt decision making might suggest. In reality I was uncomfortably aware of my lack of experience in actual combat. Nevertheless the decisions had to be made, and I made them.

It was time to meet my key subordinate leaders. I turned to the radiotelephone operator (RTO in military shorthand), the man who carried the platoon radio and whose place was always within a few feet of the leader. His name was Phil Nail. "Go get me the platoon sergeant and the squad leaders," I said. It was my first order, and it sounded good. The words came out clear and firm—not abrupt, but matter-of-fact. I was gaining some composure. It occurred to me that I might be able to pull this off after all.

While I waited I took out a can of peaches from a box of C rations. Except for the canned ham and eggs—which, when eaten cold, tasted like coagulated grease—the peaches were the closest approximation to a breakfast dish the army field rations had to offer.

As I ate, Phil Nail returned. "They'll be here in a minute," he said. He was friendly looking. Straw-colored hair shot straight up from his head; freckles covered his face and shoulders. He began to root around a pile of ration cans, studiously inspecting the fine print on their tops. He was not going to be the one to strike up a conversation. He wanted me to reveal myself first. I decided to wait. My first words would be with the sergeants.

John Hernandez, the platoon sergeant, arrived. He was a swarthy, wiry Mexican-American who came from Texas by way of Denver, Colorado. He had been in the army since the Korean War and was the only long-term professional soldier in the platoon. The war in Vietnam was decimating the NCO ranks. Those who did not become casualties on their first tour were returning to take their chances for a second and even a third time. In the combat units the odds were heavily stacked against a wound-free tour. Many of the surviving NCOs were hanging on for twenty years and retirement, but if the remaining time to twenty years was too long, many were opting to resign before the retirement date. After all, retirement held no benefits for the dead or the crippled.

Sergeant Hernandez was close to retirement. He was not about to ruin that opportunity by stopping a round with a rash move. He was steady enough, but he was at that stage where discretion was the better part of valor: "Let the war come to me" was his attitude. He was not going to go looking for it.

I knew Hernandez. He had been a "lane grader" (military jargon for an instructor) on one of my patrols in Ranger School. The night he joined us in northern Florida for his twenty-four-hour stint as an assistant ranger instructor had been a particularly nasty one. The ranger students had already been on patrol for five straight days. A cold snap had turned the swamps into a frozen nightmare. In this phase of the operation we were to cross the fast-running Yellow River. The air temperature as we reached the banks at 2300 was dropping to the low 20s. The only way to cross was to use a rope bridge, which meant total immersion in the icy water, moving hand over hand along a rope stretched just above the water's surface. I remembered Hernandez's voice that night as he sat in the darkness waiting to be the last to cross behind the ranger file. I was to take down the rope and swim the river to rejoin the patrol, so I waited with him through the painstakingly slow crossing. "How many to go?" he kept asking in the cold darkness, the rising pitch of his voice betraying his concern for the discomfort he was about to experience. Clearly, he dreaded the icy water as much as any of the ranger students, even though by dawn he would be replaced by another lane grader while the students continued for several more days on their miserable patrols. What was important, however, was that Hernandez crossed the river. He would show the same studied caution as my platoon sergeant. He did not relish looking for a fight, but when one came to him, he would do what had to be done.

"Good morning, sir," Hernandez said. He didn't remember me. I returned his greeting as the three squad leaders joined us. All were young, twenty or twenty-one years old. Sergeant James, sandy-haired and thin, from Valdosta, Georgia, looked like a young boy. He greeted me cheerfully and eagerly. Sergeant Bradshaw, from North Carolina, was more withdrawn. Small and dark, he sported a bushy mustache that accentuated his disheveled, haggard looks and made him seem old beyond his years. Sergeant Donne was the most impressive of the group. A large man with a thick head and rich, dark hair, he exuded an air of confidence. He was from Stateline, Kentucky, and was the only draftee in the platoon. Originally trained as an administrative clerk because of his two years of college, he had tired of that type of work and had volunteered to be a paratrooper because of the extra $55 a month it gave him. He had taken naturally to his position as squad leader. He was easily the biggest man in the platoon, and although soft-spoken, he was articulate and firm.

Donne, I was to learn quickly, had become the de facto leader of the platoon. Lieutenant Rolfe, my predecessor, had done throughout his entire tour what he had done on his last night in the field: nothing. Hernandez was too cautious to become the platoon's tactical leader. He would pass out supplies and check the men for personal hygiene, but he would not lead them out to face the enemy. Donne, recognizing the need for a concerted plan of action, had in his quiet way directed the patrol missions, seen to the defense of the perimeter, and supervised the control of the village.

With the four sergeants present, I began to lay down my guidelines. Within the squads, the standard operating procedures would continue until I had a chance to observe what was being done and decide if any changes were needed. I would give the platoon orders, and the sergeants, in turn, would give their own implementing orders to each member of their squads. I stated that their tactical orders would follow the standard army five-paragraph field order, specifically addressing the situation, the mission, the concept of operations, the support that could be expected, and the command and control arrangements.

Eyebrows were raised and I knew what the sergeants were thinking: they had a lieutenant who did things by the book. They realized that could be both good and bad. I could see Hernandez watching me keenly. He was probably wondering how long I would last and how much damage I would do before I went. Donne looked surprised but seemed relieved that he did not have another platoon leader who would hide in the hole frequented by his predecessor. James was scribbling notes on a ragged piece of paper he had pulled from his pocket. Bradshaw appeared to be asleep. Nail, in the background, was quietly cooking his C rations over a heat tab, absorbed in his task but no doubt hanging on every word.

"All right, men, if there are no further questions, Sergeant James will take out a reconnaissance patrol at 1300; Sergeant Donne will take his squad out right after James's return. Sergeant Bradshaw, you will place a night ambush three hundred meters to the south, on the edge of this clearing I see indicated on the map."

"Ain't no clearing there," slurred Bradshaw. "Dinks put in a potato field. Use it for a shit-hole while they work the paddies next to it. Stinks to high heaven."

This was Bradshaw's subtle way of telling the new lieutenant he did not know anything. I was ready for him. "Okay, set up in the potato field," I told him. "It should be easy to find in the dark. I'll join you." And to James: "Let me know when you're ready to give your operations order. I want to hear it because I'll be going out of the wire with you."

"Sergeant Hernandez, while I'm gone, keep Nail and his radio next to you. If I need to reach you, I'll use the squad radio." The orders given, the men moved off. I tried to doze for a few minutes before inspecting the perimeter. *That should keep them guessing*, I thought smugly.

A fly buzzed lazily over my face. It seemed to know that my attempt at sleep was only a sham. My heart was racing in time with its beating wings. My nerves had gone taut, for I knew that soon I must begin the irreversible first step toward my first combat patrol. It didn't occur to me then that the irreversible step had been taken years ago in some forgotten moment of my childhood. Beads of sweat trickled from my neck down the length of my back to drip onto the smothering flak jacket. The fly buzzed away, indifferent to my plight.

The patrol preparations were carried out smoothly. Sergeant James gave his squad the operations order with some self-consciousness about my presence in the background. The men needed little coaching, however, in readying their gear for the patrol, and precisely at 1300 we moved out through the wire.

My expectations were similar to those I had upon landing at Bien Hoa airport. I braced myself for incoming rounds the moment I stepped beyond the perimeter, only to be amazed at the lush peacefulness of the countryside. It seemed as if I was just along for the ride, but it was a learning process for me. I watched how the men moved, how they dispersed, how alert they seemed, and what they carried. I also watched the terrain. How treacherous it seemed. The rice paddies were virtually impassable; the only convenient way across them was the dikes—dirt mounds that afforded walkways no more than a foot wide. Contiguous to the paddies was underbrush offering good concealment for an enemy. Walking across the paddies was like setting yourself up as a moving target in a shooting gallery. The single files made necessary by the dikes were convenient targets for an enemy in the bushes along the edge of the paddy.

Where there were no paddies there were heavy undergrowth, narrow trails, high grass, abrupt slopes, and generally inhospitable terrain. Wherever it was easy to walk, you could expect booby traps. Where the trails narrowed, you could expect to be ambushed. This was not the terrain for conventional tactics. Movement was slow. Anyone moving was at a disadvantage. Anyone waiting could bide his time. The countryside was beautiful but, for us Americans, very unfriendly.

Even more awe-inspiring than the scenery was the realization that whatever took place in this part of the world, whatever these men did or whatever happened to them, was my responsibility. I might describe myself as "along for the ride," but whatever happened here or back at the perimeter I would have to account for—to my superiors, to my men, and to myself. I felt I was living a lie: I was trying desperately to learn what I was already supposed to know.

The soldiers looked good. They moved with a purpose, weapons held high and at the ready. They looked sharply at the ground to their front and flanks, each man apparently picking up his own primary sector of responsibility. For a moment I thought they were putting on a good show for me but then I realized they were not acting. This was for real. As in my first boxing match, I was becoming aware that there were people in this arena who meant to hurt me as badly as they could. I raised my guard a bit.

Thankfully, I was not challenged the first time out. It was a quiet patrol. We passed a few peasants working the fields, but nothing more. Although I breathed easier at the end, I knew that my challenge would come soon enough.

Back at the platoon base I busied myself learning more about the tactical position and the personality of the men. There was a distance between us in those first hours. I was not sure of their soldierliness and they were not sure of my leadership. I sent out a second patrol in the afternoon. They reported sighting a fleeing Viet Cong and fired a few futile shots after him. I wondered what was happening out there. Why were they seeing something, when I had seen nothing on my patrol?

I prepared myself for the night ambush going out after midnight. This elicited some surprise from the men. Apparently they did not expect officers to go out on night patrols; perhaps they felt the experience would be unpleasant. Nevertheless, they extended to me the respect due my position and said nothing. I was a little anxious as the sun went down, knowing that I would be moving out there in the darkness when only the night before I had spent the entire time lying in a hole beside the outgoing platoon leader.

Patrolling at night is a unique experience. Although I had done it countless times in training, the knowledge that there truly were things in the darkness that sought to do me terrible harm brought back a childhood fear. It was downright scary. I felt certain the enemy could see our every move as clear as day while we groped blindly in the ominous darkness. The sounds we made seemed magnified in the warm night air, as if we were purposely signaling our location. Every twig that snapped, every leaf or blade of grass that rustled, seemed to shout our whereabouts. And all the time the enemy sat in his inky black silence, waiting for us to blunder into his deadly trap.

In reality, the night is neutral, but it was hard for me to believe that as we moved to our position. At the appointed place the gruff squad leader Bradshaw placed each of us in position on line. Although I was tense at first, the quiet waiting, each of us alone in his own dark world, began to relax me.

The day had been long and demanding. As I lay on my stomach, weapon in hand, my wakefulness slipped away. It was uncanny. Even as I waited to kill someone, my head kept nodding as if I were drifting off to a peaceful sleep in the security of my childhood bed. It was the fear of embarrassment at being found asleep by my soldiers, not the fear of the enemy, that kept me awake. Thankfully, the dawn came without incident, and I could move back to the security of the platoon perimeter without having been tested.

On the morning of the second day I began to assert myself more as a platoon leader. I critiqued the patrol I had accompanied on ambush, pointing out the several mistakes that had been made in setting up. Hypocritically, I criticized the men for getting sleepy in the ambush site. I also began to order improvements in the defensive line, and I made my first official visit to the village of which I was virtually the military commander. I gave the operations order for the patrol that was to go out at 1300. I would accompany it. I would be going on my third combat patrol within forty-eight hours of assuming leadership of the platoon.

The uniform for the platoon was standard operating procedure. As we were patrolling only for short periods of time in the vicinity of our platoon base, there was no need to take the traditional rucksack with its extra clothing, extra water, and portions of the platoon basic load. Instead, each man wore a flak jacket, a protective vest that would be too cumbersome to wear with a rucksack. Although the jacket was hot and constraining, it was bearable. Each man carried his own ammunition for his basic weapon, which was normally the M-16 rifle. Since the ammunition was lightweight, a great amount of it was carried. For example, as the platoon leader (the most lightly armed man in the platoon), I carried about twenty-five magazines loaded with eighteen rounds each (every fifth one a tracer round). Additionally, each man carried several fragmentation grenades (for killing) and several smoke grenades (for signaling). At least two light antitank weapons were carried by the squad, and I gradually increased that so that eventually each man carried one. A machine gun might or might not be included on patrol. If the M-60 machine gun was carried, then the links of ammunition, which were much heavier than those for the M-16, were broken down among the squad members. Each man carried either an army issue bayonet or his personal knife. For ambushes, claymore mines would be added to the arsenal. Additionally, the leaders were outfitted with various flares of assorted color and type, as well as with the necessary map and compass and the nearby radio hefted by the stalwart radio man, the RTO.

Rounding out the soldier's fighting gear was his trusty steel helmet. It was cursed by the soldier for its weight and awkwardness, but was worth its weight in gold for its protective value. Finally came the functional web gear: belt, suspenders, ammunition pouches, canteen covers, and first aid pouches. By all standards, we were very well equipped. Nonetheless, I felt quite naked as we started out of the wire on my third patrol in the Republic of Vietnam.

# CHAPTER 6

# THE WOUNDING

Right from the beginning, I had an inkling that things would be different on this patrol. It was a beautiful day; the sky was perfectly clear and there was a gentle breeze. The countryside was picturesque, a mosaic of well-kept paddies and potato fields occasionally interrupted by the stooping, swaying peasants at their daily toil. The pastoral scene did not reassure me. I knew it was only a matter of time. Two quiet patrols were as much of a grace period as I could expect. A slight sweat began working its way down between my shoulder blades.

Twenty minutes out of the wire, the point man stopped suddenly, dropping to one knee and raising his hand in the designated signal to halt. We were in single file, the standard method of movement in this part of Vietnam; it lowered the chances of hitting a booby trap. Walking third, I stooped down and peered toward the front, seeing nothing more ominous than two elderly Vietnamese working a corner of a potato patch about two hundred meters ahead. I watched for a moment but saw nothing else. Threateningly, the point man raised his M-16 and pointed it in the direction of the old man, quickly flicking the weapon's safety to the fire position. Confused, I said nothing, but memories of accusations of wanton killing in Vietnam began stirring in my mind.

Sergeant Donne hunkered over the point man, then

waved his huge hand in an upward motion. Obediently the point man arose and moved on in the direction we had been traveling, oblivious of the two men he was awaiting an order to shoot only seconds ago.

The scene repeated itself several times as we wound through the countryside. Donne's control of his squad was reassuring. The men trusted him, reacting smoothly to his orders, orders given less by voice than by shrugs, motions, and facial expressions. Donne was taking no chances, but he was bothering no one unless he had to. I was glad he knew his business so well. I quite frankly did not know what was going on.

At about 1345, as we came up over a little rise, we saw two figures bending over a mound in the dirt about one hundred twenty-five meters away. This time when the point man alerted, the squad leader shifted the squad on line. The soldiers moved silently, each switching his weapon to fire. I took a hard look at the figures. One was a man of indeterminate age, perhaps thirty, but then again perhaps fifty—the jet black Vietnamese hair and the distance between him and us made it impossible to tell. The other figure was a small boy, maybe eight years of age, perhaps the son of the older man. It occurred to me that the squad was about to shoot them.

I turned to Donne and uttered my first words of the mission: "What are you doing?"

The sergeant's reply was short: "VC."

I felt it was time for me to assert myself. I would not allow the squad to fire. I did not see any weapons, and regardless of the political leanings of the older man, the boy, to my way of thinking, deserved a little more consideration.

"Hold off," I said to Donne. His look spoke a thousand words. He wasn't accustomed to being second-guessed. Not only had he been a squad leader, he had been leading the entire platoon. And now I was challenging him.

My decision was made and I couldn't back away. If I relinquished my command, the squad would open fire; both man and boy were as good as dead. Maybe Donne was right. What did I know? I was the newcomer. If I let him give the orders, the consequences were his. If I gave the orders, they were mine.

No, I decided, either way the consequences were mine. I was the senior man; even if I looked the other way, I would have sanctioned the killing. I stared back at Donne.

"If they're VC, we'll try to take them alive," I said.

Again came the wave of the big hand. The squad arose and quietly began to close the distance to the two figures. Donne was a good soldier. He did not like the order, but he followed it.

Before we had covered fifty meters the two Vietnamese heard us coming and darted into the heavy brush at the end of the field where they were working. For a few minutes we followed in pursuit, but the flak jackets took their toll in the sweltering heat. We could not maintain the pace. We returned to ranger file and attempted to follow our quarry more deliberately. I fell back into line in the number four position with three men behind me. Once again I was just a member of the patrol. I knew that my first combat order may have looked a little foolish. Nonetheless, I was glad we had not killed the boy.

I sensed a slight pull on my right foot, and pivoting to my left I took a broad step.

The roaring in my left ear was tremendous. As if in a dream, I began floating in the direction of my last step. It was still a warm, beautifully clear day, yet somehow I didn't seem to be there anymore. I was going off into a deep sleep, although my eyes were wide open and

I could see the soldiers in front of me exactly as they had been a moment ago. I continued to float. How graceful I felt. Sensing everything in slow motion, I saw the ground rising to meet my chest. What a perfect landing it was, the ground sliding up underneath me. Then I rose again, rebounding from the impact in a billow of soft, fine dust particles. Again I eased down into the dirt, sending a second, thicker cloud of brown debris rising around my face and outstretched hands.

Abruptly, the pace of my thoughts quickened as the surrealistic effects left: "My God, we've been hit!" Then the pace increased to normal: "Oh, no, it's me." I felt sick to my stomach. I thought I would vomit, and I made my first deliberate movement since the explosion had gone off in my ear. From my prone position, I jerked my head to the left and gaped at my legs. *Oh, be there! Please be there!*

They were there, bleeding and torn, but there. I was so happy I wanted to shout with joy. I was euphoric. But the realization that I was hurt settled back into my numbed brain. There was still no pain. *Why doesn't it hurt? It's supposed to hurt, isn't it? Then why don't I hurt?*

Maybe two seconds had passed since the explosion. Medical reports would later identify it as a 155-millimeter artillery shell, set up as a booby trap with a trip wire and a delay fuse. My guess is that it was much smaller, perhaps a 60-millimeter mortar round. By turning to my left I had kept it from exploding between my legs. I am not sure that I really knew I had tripped a booby trap. I just decided to step aside at that particular point in time. The line between skill and luck in combat is not very well defined.

At perhaps the third second I felt pain for the first time. Shrapnel is hot, and where it was embedded under my skin, I was being burned. My insides were on fire.

Somehow I was being scorched, but I couldn't pull away from the flames. Suddenly my fear returned.

Then I remembered that I was the leader. I braced myself as if I were about to jump into icy water. Concern for myself would have to come later. Three men were moving toward me, and I ordered them back, yelling for a report on how many others were hurt. I could hear no reply. *I could not hear.*

I motioned for one man to come to me, and I repeated my question to him. By shouting in my right ear he told me I was the only casualty. I ordered the squad leader to set up a defensive perimeter, then allowed the soldier next to me to begin working on me. I could see the blood coming from my left thigh, right knee, and left arm. I felt blood on my left buttock, but could not see back there. My clothes were torn, my helmet was blown off (there was a gash on the left side of the steel casing), and my flak jacket was half-on, half-off, hanging in shreds. The shrapnel had punched through the flak jacket but had only slightly penetrated my left side, which was as bruised as if someone had hit it with a baseball bat. The most frightening wound was in my head. Blood was flowing down the left side of my face into my left eye, and the whole left side of my skull was ringing. I asked the soldier how bad it was. In the Vietnamese-American jargon of the infantryman he replied, "*Ti-ti,*" meaning "a little." "You'll be all right," he said, "but your left ear is missing."

I had a sinking feeling. I envisioned how grotesque I would look with an ear gone, a modern-day Van Gogh. But then I reassured myself. Ears were only cosmetic things, and they didn't matter anyway if you couldn't hear out of them—which I couldn't do out of my left one. (As it turned out, the soldier was wrong. My ear was still there, but it was matted and covered with blood and mud.)

A wounded leader is still a leader, unless so incapacitated he can't make decisions. I wasn't that bad off,
and I found it somewhat consoling to assert myself as
the man in charge. At the very least, it staved off the
shock that would come later.

For the American wounded, Vietnam was the best
of our wars. If you lived until the arrival of the medical
evacuation helicopter (medevac), you were probably
going to make it. That helicopter was protected from
enemy fire only by international law, which was not
well observed in Vietnam. I was lucky. I had the soldiers
secure a landing zone, and within fifteen minutes of
being wounded I was on my way to medical aid. My last
command act was to give the squad instructions for returning to base and to designate the chain of command
in my absence.

I was taken to a forward aid station located at LZ
English, the headquarters of the 173d. There the remaining clothes were removed from my body, my boots
were cut away, and I was literally doused, as I lay on a
stretcher, with antiseptics. My head dressing was tightened and I received a shot of morphine to kill the pain.
Then I was moved to the rear to make room for the
treatment of other wounded.

Lying naked on a stretcher suspended between two
chairs, I began to suffer the first sensations of shock. I
began to shake severely and thought once again I was
going to vomit. I also was afraid of defecating where I
lay. I was so overcome with self-pity that for a second I
caught myself starting to shed a tear. The morphine was
having its effect, and I was not in full control of my
emotions.

More than anything, I was scared. I was no longer
afraid that I would die; I was afraid because I could
have died. My heart was racing; my body was trem-
bling. The ringing in my ear confused my drugged

thinking even more, and I couldn't focus my thoughts. I only knew I had completely failed in my first attempt to lead a combat action. The West Pointer, the paratrooper, the ranger—he had lasted less than forty-eight hours, blown up by his own blundering footwork and ill-considered decisions. How inglorious it all seemed, lying there in my nakedness.

Fate never stands still. The enemy chose that moment to unleash a mortar barrage on the aid station, giving me something else to think about. The numbers of wounded had steadily increased while I lay helplessly on my stretcher, and one by one we were carried or helped to an underground bunker. Although rounds were coming in erratically, well off the mark, it was not prudent to risk a lucky hit.

I was placed among a group of wounded in a half-lit corner of the bunker. At last, the shakes had left me. A soldier sitting beside me tried to strike up a conversation. Despite the morphine clouding my thinking, I knew in an instant he was completely out of his head. He was either suffering from combat fatigue or was so laced with self-inflicted drugs that he could only babble incoherently.

"Hey, man," he drooled, "don't worry. I won't let them get you."

I looked away.

"It's okay. I'll kill them; I already killed a lot of them," he went on.

"Those are mortars," I said.

"Yeah, I already killed a lot of them," he said. The conversation was going no place. I was relieved to see he wasn't armed.

No one was paying attention to us. Medical orderlies were busy running back and forth, shifting more and more wounded into the bunker.

"Don't worry," my new friend continued. "Hey, you really been hit, man. You're all messed up!"

*Look who's talking!* I thought.

"Hey, it's all right, buddy. Take it easy."

I tried to look indifferent.

"I'll cover you with my body" was his next offer.

"That's all right," I said, wishing I had some clothes on. "Look, I'm okay. Take care of yourself."

He smiled.

"Don't worry about me," I said.

Seeing a medic enter the bunker with yet another wounded soldier, I called to him. "Get this son of a bitch away from me," I shouted, my voice rising in panic.

"He won't hurt you."

"Get him away, goddamn it!"

My protector must have been offended. He moved away, but I kept a wary eye on him. The medic gave me a blanket. I felt better.

At the end of the shelling I was lifted on my stretcher and moved to a helicopter that would take me to the hospital in Qui Nhon. Four other wounded soldiers came aboard. One was gut-shot, and about four inches of his stomach were poking out of his middle. He shielded his wound with his hands as he walked out to the chopper. The other ambulatory patient had an AK-47 round lodged in his left arm. Compared to the rest of us, he seemed relatively spry. The other two were carried on stretchers. I didn't know what their wounds were.

I was placed on the upper rack of the helicopter, my face only a few inches from the padded ceiling. If dead men could see, that must be the view they'd get from inside a coffin. My mind drifted back to the boy and the man. Were they the ones who nearly killed me? Should I have been so careful for their lives? Was I now a victim of my own idealism? Did my soldiers think me a fool? My mind raced over those questions, then found some

peace in the reflection that, no, I should not have fired
and, no, I would not fire if the situation arose again.

I was jerked from my thoughts abruptly as the
bandage around my head began to unravel in the wind
rushing into the open helicopter. The sticky red-and-
white streamer snaked out the door, and I feared that
my head would be jerked off if the bandage was
snapped up by the helicopter rotors. I tried desperately
to get the attention of the medic. He was busy with the
gut-shot soldier, his back turned to my feeble cries for
help, my voice unheard above the rush of the wind.
Later, I would realize that my fears were unrealistic. The
down-draft from the blades made it physically impossible for the wrappings to be caught up. But at the moment I believed it possible.

The real shocks were yet to come at Qui Nhon.
There the commotion reminded me of the Battle of At-
lanta scenes in *Gone with the Wind*. Wounded were
being brought in from all over Military Region II, the
wide-ranging area surrounding the hospital at Qui
Nhon. One American armored cavalry platoon had just
been ambushed in the "506 Valley" south of Bong Son,
and nine bloated and charred—but still alive—soldiers
were brought in and placed next to me. They smelled
awful, and their pain was excruciating. Mercifully, some
were unconscious, but those awake were screaming. The
violent shaking I had experienced at LZ English was
rampant among the group. I was grateful to be an infantryman. I wouldn't want to travel in gasoline-fed ma-
chines that invariably exploded and burned when hit.

Presently another group of wounded, this time Vietnamese, was brought in. There were so many patients
that the hospital was forced to give its attention first to
the most seriously wounded who had a chance to survive. Those likely to die or the lightly wounded were
treated later.

The nurse who prepared me for surgery was new at her job and the day had obviously been a strain on her. She repeatedly attempted to penetrate my veins with an intravenous injection; after the fifth attempt she berated me for puny veins. Apologizing, I explained that I had bled a lot, which consoled her a bit. Feeling sorry for her, I coached her on the next four attempts. By then, however, she was crying. Eventually, a doctor came by and made an incision in my left ankle to complete the IV.

After the preparation, there was another long wait for an operating table. A Vietnamese soldier had been brought in and placed ahead of me, signifying the greater severity of his wounds. He too had been gut-shot, and apparently his stomach and intestines had completely spilled out. His stomach lay quite exposed, but his intestines, still attached, had been dumped into a sandbag which was securely tied to his thigh. When he was brought in he was unconscious, but after a while he came to. I saw him lift his head and stare at the sandbag. What he saw made him pass out again. The cycle of coming to, looking at his intestines, and passing out was repeated three times. On the last go-around he must have died, for he was abruptly removed from line and taken away from the operating room.

My last recollection was of being placed on the operating table and rolled over roughly by a middle-aged nurse. Despite my stupor, I clearly remember that she was very upset about not being informed appropriately that it was her turn to go on shift. I felt no sympathy for her.

# CHAPTER 7

# BRIEF INTERLUDE

I awoke on clean sheets. The sensation was reassuring; maybe all the recent events had been a bad dream. Maybe I was home in bed.

But no, on either side of me and across the large open room were rows of beds and patients wrapped in bandages. It had not been a dream.

Time to check myself out. *Everything there—fingers, toes, arms, legs. What about that ear?* It was hard to tell with bandages thickly wadded over the left side of my head. I still couldn't hear anything over there except a constant ringing. *Wait, there it is.* I could feel it, my ear, pressing up against the dressing! *Thank my lucky stars!*

As it turned out, I was relatively lightly wounded. For the first day or two after the shrapnel was removed, there was talk about evacuating me to Japan, but by the third day it was apparent I was healing nicely. I could tell that as quickly from the attitude of the chaplains as I could from the doctors. The latter were trying to get me out of there and the former were becoming more concerned about my living than my dying. Mercifully, both groups soon lost interest and left me alone.

I wanted to get out of bed. A bedpan is an awkward instrument, and besides, I wanted to place a call to my wife. It was better for her to get the news straight from me. I could edit appropriately.

My first steps were shaky, so I decided to take a test run and headed for the latrine, wheeling my IV with me. I pushed myself too hard and passed out ignominiously at a urinal.

Before long I was able to maneuver myself to an overseas telephone, wait in line, and call my wife.

"Hi Pat, this is Jim . . . Oh, I'm fine, how are you? Well, I'm calling just to say hello. Actually I'm not really fine. You see, I had a little accident . . . No, no—I'm not really hurt. Well, yes, I was wounded, but it's not so bad. It's like being a little sick, really. It doesn't even hurt . . . Oh, no, I'm not missing anything. Honest— just a few scratches . . .

"Pat, don't cry. I'm really not hurt. I just called so you wouldn't be upset if the army told you. It's barely worth mentioning . . . Well, I guess I'll go back. Oh, I am in the 173d Airborne Brigade. You can write me there. The address will be on the first letter I wrote after I got there . . .

"No, don't worry. It's a pretty quiet unit. They have what's called a pacification mission. Not much action; we just kind of protect the people as they go about their business . . . Well, I guess I've got to go. Oh, Pat, please tell my parents. I don't want them to hear rumors. Tell them I'm okay. I'll write in a letter exactly the extent of the wounds—I mean injuries . . .

"Pat, I love you. Don't cry, I'm really fine. Pat, I miss you. I love you, honey, good-bye."

Reluctantly I hung up the phone, severing the fragile link with the world of sanity, security, and love. I returned to the present. A black soldier shuffled up to the telephone. He was in a cast from his waist to his neck, his left arm propped up at a ninety-degree angle from his shoulder in yet another cast. He looked preoccupied, as if he were trying to compose the words he would use to reassure the folks back home. That phone must have sent a lot of lies.

Life in the hospital wasn't too bad, and for a few days I could forget the war. I visited with some of the soldiers who had come in with me. The boy with the stomach wound felt lucky. His stomach was still protruding from his midriff, but odds were against his going back into combat. The boy with a round lodged in his arm had had surgery, and he felt it was bad luck that his wound was healing so nicely that he would soon be back out in the bush. He even beat me back to the field.

Sergeant Bradshaw arrived on the fifth day of my stay. He had been picked off by a sniper while standing inside the platoon perimeter. He was in serious condition; I visited him in the intensive care unit. His dark face had lost its tough, grizzled look. His body seemed shriveled, smaller than I remembered; only his eyes looked large, perhaps swollen with fear.

"Hello, sarge," I greeted him.

He responded weakly, "Hello, lieutenant. I heard you was dead."

"Nope," I smiled. "How are you feeling?"

"Not so good. But I'm going to make it," he answered, the toughness showing through.

We talked a while. He seemed in remarkably good spirits for a man who had almost been killed. He told me he had been talking about his family when it happened. He had reached into his rucksack and pulled out a Bible in which he had neatly pressed pictures of his children. As he extended his arm to show off the photographs, the sniper caught him in the left side, the bullet ricocheting off a bone and exiting through his chest. The lung was punctured, leaving a sucking chest wound in the bullet's wake.

I regretted that I would not get to know Sergeant

Bradshaw. Away from the confines of the platoon, he let his defenses down. "You really don't look like a platoon leader," he confided.

I was disappointed. Secretly I felt I had not been much of a platoon leader, but I at least wanted to look the part.

"Nah, you look like you should be something else, like maybe a banker. Yeah, a small-town banker. You look like you should carry a briefcase, not all that shit you got to carry out there." Bradshaw was destroying my self-image, but he didn't mean any harm. He was wishing me safer environs. At the end of our talk he cautioned me.

"Don't go back there," he said. "If you can find a way out, take it. I ain't seen an officer out there yet who was worth a damn that made it. Just like you, they all got hit trying to do what they're supposed to. Only the pukes, like that guy Rolfe, make it. And all they do is screw up a lot of good men looking out for themselves." Bradshaw was tired now, and I let him get some sleep. He had his ticket home. The next day he was evacuated to Japan and, I heard later, from there to the United States. "Back to the world," as the saying went.

On day number seven a very nervous officer from the adjutant general corps stopped by my bed. He had been reprimanded by a superior for falling behind in issuing his orders. I signed his form acknowledging my receipt of a Purple Heart, and he moved down the row of beds, dispersing his burdensome medals. I mailed the orders and the medal to my wife, who would be terribly impressed. The following day a general came by and gave me a cigarette lighter inscribed "To a Wounded Sky Soldier." No matter that I didn't smoke.

Surely, getting wounded was not so bad after all. Nonetheless, I was getting bored in the hospital. I had long since stopped trying to make the pretty nurses feel sorry for me. They were much too busy, and I hardly qualified as more than a routine case. The constant flow of wounded—American and Vietnamese, soldiers and civilians, men and women, adults and children—was depressing. Each day I steeled myself a little more for my return to combat. With my stitches still in, I checked out of the hospital on the twentieth day and once again made my way by truck and by helicopter back up to LZ North English. Pending the removal of the stitches, I was assigned the relatively safe job of night duty officer in the tactical command and control bunker. My job was to monitor the radio communications of the ambushes and patrols of the battalion units in the field. If anything critical happened, I was to awaken the battalion commander or the operations officer. It gave me something to do while I waited for my wounds to finish healing. I could keep them clean there too; out in the field they could get infected.

I could sense that I was inching my way toward the front again. (Actually, the term "front" was wholly inappropriate for Vietnam. The front was everywhere beyond the few enclaves held by Vietnamese or American government forces. In Vietnam, the term "bush" was a more accurate description of where the enemy was to be met.) Out in the bush, the battalion established its squad-size patrols. During my final days of healing, as I monitored the situations that developed for those exposed elements, I had ample time to reflect on what it might be like to return to my platoon.

One of the attractions of military service, which admittedly has a number of features that would otherwise deter men of sound reason, is the number of challenges it offers. The challenge to overcome personal fear is one of the more seductive sirens. It is a deeply internalized struggle. Fear itself is not shameful. In fact, the absence of fear in the face of combat would be a suspicious

abnormality of character. The challenge lies in not deny-
ing fear, but in being able to function in the face of it.
Having been slightly hurt and having been exposed to a
variety of broken bodies during my stay in the hospital,
I knew I would have to cope with my fears in order to
be an effective platoon leader. I had been lucky the first
time; my next break from combat would come only
as a result of death, a severe wound, or a long run of
good luck. My state of mind had changed since I arrived
in Vietnam. I now knew that I, like everyone else, was
vulnerable.

I began to plan how I would confront my fears
when I returned to the field. Like a man facing the
prospect of entering icy water, I had two alternatives:
ease myself in gradually or jump in with a big splash.

The sounds over the radio were ominous. Every
night something happened. Long periods of silence were
broken by sudden interruptions of fierce contacts, followed by the evacuation of casualties. I remembered
many a night as a teenager sitting at ringside, waiting
for my bout to come up on the card, watching the mayhem that preceded me. That was the sensation I felt as
the hours passed, bringing me ever closer to the violence
that awaited. Soon it would be my turn again.

A visit one night by a young, enthusiastic lieutenant
on his way back to the States was a welcome break in
the routine. He came in to talk because he was too excited to sleep. He couldn't believe his good fortune at
coming to the end of his tour, alive and well. Almost
every lieutenant who had arrived with him a year earlier
had long since departed, dead or wounded. Now he had
only to wait until morning for a helicopter to Camranh
Bay and the airplane that would take him back home to
the girl who was waiting to marry him. I had never met
such a happy man.

As we talked, the lieutenant drank beer after beer,

now and then commenting on the fate of the poor devils out on patrol. Around midnight the beer had collected in his bladder and he excused himself, promising to come back in a moment and tell me more about the wonderful girl he would soon be seeing. I envied him as he walked out the door.

A few seconds later a muffled explosion echoed through the walls of the bunker. I guessed it was an incoming mortar round.

"Stay put," I cautioned the two radio men in the bunker with me. There was no use walking out into a mortar barrage. Seconds passed; there were no more explosions. I hoped the lieutenant was all right. Maybe he had been able to get down when the first round hit. That would have been the smart thing to do. Then, if no more mortars came in he could make a dash to the door. A minute passed. I decided to go out and see what had happened.

At that instant, the bunker door was kicked open. I was standing ten feet from the portal, and I was splattered in the face by a burst of blood. The lieutenant stood there, his jugular vein exposed and split wide, the blood squirting wickedly from his throat with each beat of his heart. He tried to speak, but only an inarticulate gurgle came from his torn throat. His eyes were gaping in horror, trying to express what his lips could not. In his hands were his spilled intestines. I knew what he was thinking: *It can't be happening to me, not on the eve of my departure.*

I ignored his gaping abdomen and reached for his neck to try to stop the heavy bleeding. He had fallen to the floor at the door, his face pleading with me to save him. Blood was gushing from his neck. I was trying not to be overcome by the revulsion I was feeling. *Keep cool,* I kept telling myself. *There must be something I can do.*

I ripped the undershirt from the nearest RTO and placed it directly over the lieutenant's neck. It was useless. Within seconds, the green T-shirt was a rose red. The lieutenant was grabbing at me, trying to speak, trying to find a way to help me help him. Grabbing his jugular with my forefinger and thumb, I tried to hold the split pieces of vein in line with each other. It seemed to help a bit; the flow of blood decreased. The bleeding was still so heavy I knew it would ultimately be fatal. As the man weakened from the loss of blood, he stopped struggling and I was able to get a better alignment on his torn jugular. Although it was a slippery business, I managed to get most of the blood flowing in its proper channel. After a few minutes, a medic arrived and did a much better job. Eventually a helicopter arrived and took the lieutenant to the hospital from which I had so recently returned.

I heard later that the man survived, although it took a great many transfusions to get him through the night. Whether or not that is true, I don't know. In Vietnam, once the wounded were evacuated, it was as if they disappeared from the surface of the earth. The only way we knew what happened to them was if they came back. Usually they didn't.

And what had blown my new friend apart the night before he was home free? It was not an enemy mortar attack. The lieutenant had gone to the bunkered hootch of the battalion sergeant major. As the officer stood there in the darkness urinating against the sandbags, a soldier chose that moment to let the sergeant major know how he felt about him by tossing a hand grenade at his hootch. The soldier claimed later that he never saw the lieutenant, that he never intended to hurt anybody. He only wanted to scare the sergeant major.

I learned that night that you were never "out of it" in Vietnam. You could never let your guard down. The

Grim Reaper was everywhere and the odds were on his side. Let up for a minute, and he would get you.

My prep school training had been completed. I had gone to the field, met my unit, and abruptly left, soaked in blood. Now, on the verge of my return to the field, I had been soaked in blood again. On my first entry in the field I had been wide-eyed and somewhat in awe of the fate that awaited me. Now I was better prepared for whatever might come. I had been forced to make an adjustment to my new environment. I had been socialized to the ways of war. Although I was still a stranger to combat—after all, I had only stepped on a booby trap, not been engaged in a firefight—I knew that the game was played for keeps. I had been fortunate. My education may have been harsh, but it wasn't fatal. This time I wasn't going to wonder about my fate. I was going to try to control it.

# CHAPTER 8

# IF AT FIRST YOU DON'T SUCCEED . . .

Returning to my "old platoon" after being wounded gave me a few advantages I would not otherwise have had. I was not the green soldier I had been a few weeks ago, at least not from the men's point of view. I was not only a veteran; I was a wounded veteran. Moreover, the very fact that I returned was impressive to men conditioned to thinking the worst. Soldiers love to exaggerate, and because of the stories circulated about the extent of my wounds, many had believed me dead. Those who did not assumed that I was permanently disabled. Consequently they were surprised to see me alighting from the helicopter. "Must be pretty tough," their faces seemed to say, and I decided to take full advantage of their assessment.

Establishing authority over others, however, is sometimes easier than establishing authority over yourself. My first order of business was to calm the butterflies in my own stomach, but before I could do that I had to invest a little time in recovering my gear. My knife, canteens, poncho, ammunition pouches, and other equipment had been distributed among the members of the platoon upon what was presumed my permanent departure.

I placed myself with the first patrol scheduled out that night. It would be an ambush patrol, and we would travel a great distance, about twenty-five hundred meters, in the darkness. My nerves were beginning to jump as the sun went down. I donned the usual gear, no longer resenting the flak jacket and steel helmet, two items I had come to appreciate. I placed myself fourth in the order of march as we slid out of the wire. The first fifty yards were tolerable, but as we left the relative security of the perimeter farther and farther behind, I began to dread that each footstep would land me on another booby trap. I tried not to think about my wounds and the mayhem and gore I had seen during the past few weeks, but the more I tried to forget, the more clearly I remembered. I felt I was going to die, and I began to grieve—for myself, for my wife, for the little boy who would never really know his father. Sweat poured from my forehead, my back, my every joint. My stomach was as tight as a knot. Each step felt as if it might paralyze me. I tried hard to feel my legs so I would remember them long after they were blown off. I was torturing myself.

Then I realized that the other men must be afraid too. Yet they kept moving. I was their leader. I had been trained for my job in the best installations the U.S. Army had to offer—West Point, Airborne School, Ranger School, Jungle Warfare School. How could I be deficient after such an investment, while my men, wrenched from unmilitary backgrounds into the army and quickly processed in impersonal training facilities, continued to do their duty? Somehow I kept moving. I could not allow myself to appear cowardly in the eyes of those men. Besides, there was no place else to go.

We moved well. Hardly a word was spoken as we entered the ambush area from the rear. Quietly, the squad leader pointed out each man's position, making sure to designate flank and rear security. Orders were acknowledged with a slight nod of the head. The ambush was set.

We were moving in beside a trail, not far from where I had been blown up only a few weeks ago. Beneath my flak jacket I was soaking wet.

*Concentrate on what you're doing,* I kept telling myself. The rest would be fate, and there was nothing I could do about that. I felt awkward, uncoordinated—a dancer who could not dance, an artist who could not draw.

I had to go only a few more feet to reach my designated position in the ambush site. I went down on all fours, creeping in from the rear, trying not to be heard, trying not to disturb the brush beside the kill zone. The compass attached to my shoulder strap was connected by a shoelace to my web belt. As I struggled through the undergrowth, the lace caught on a branch and pulled the compass loose from its berth, causing it to fall to the ground where it struck a rock. The metallic case made a loud ping as it bounced.

Without hesitation I yelled, "Booby trap!" I lurched to the right, threw myself to the ground, covered my head with my arms, and tried to pull my legs up into my butt and brace for the explosion that was about to rip me apart. All about I could hear men thrashing away from me, sucking in their breath as if to preserve their last gasp of air. As the seconds ticked off without the expected explosion and the ripping of flesh, it dawned on me what I had done. I groped in the dark and found the compass dangling from the string still attached to my web gear. I was no longer afraid. The fear left me in a rush, replaced by an overwhelming wave of embarrassment. I had overreacted to the sound of my own compass falling from my shoulder and in so doing had compromised the ambush. My yell had endangered us more than any booby trap could have.

My outcry forced us to move to another ambush site, but there was no more excitement that night. Later on as we moved back to the platoon base in the darkness, I am sure my face was emitting a red glow. Nonetheless, I felt relieved. I had made a buffoon of myself, but that wasn't so bad. No one was hurt, and I had gotten over the terror left by my wounding.

I took the time to debrief the platoon upon reentry to the perimeter, pointing out the strong points and the weak points of the night's actions. I did not spare myself in the critique; I simply stated what had happened. I had made a mistake, but an honest one. There were a few subdued comments by the patrol members, all of whom clearly recognized the danger of my action. It didn't matter. I had overcome my fear. I was once again in control of my platoon, and, more importantly, myself.

My indoctrination period was over. I had been blooded but had survived. I had been embarrassed but would recover. The early shocks had been merciful in that they were over quickly. I could now turn my attention away from the self-conscious concerns of how I would fit into this alien environment and how I might be perceived by the soldiers I led. I could concentrate instead upon improving my style of leadership and fighting the enemy.

There was much to do. For too long the platoon had done only those things necessary to minimize casualties, an approach that in the long run would surely lead to maximum casualties. I was concerned about the lack of emphasis on the details that are the essence of tactics: defense, offense, patrolling, ambushing, weapons employment, weapons maintenance, setting mines, uncovering mines, handling prisoners, planning indirect fire support, first aid, map reading, night movement, stream crossings, and so on. They were things I understood. I had studied them in theory and practiced them for years. The only difference now was that the stakes were for real. Neglecting the small details would be costly to us. Doing them correctly would be costly to the enemy.

An old army adage claims that soldiers only do well that which their commander checks. In combat everything must be done well, yet I realized I couldn't possibly check everything. But I could create the illusion that everything was being checked, especially if I used the squad leaders and the platoon sergeant as extensions of my will.

Not only tactics, but all matters relevant to our life in the field had to be supervised. For instance, health habits had to be inspected as diligently as weapons were. Soldiers have to be kept clean. They have to shave and wash, and the squad leader has to see that they do. Soldiers need a place to relieve themselves, a place secure from both the enemy and disease. Mess equipment has to be kept clean, and soldiers need a balanced diet. Feet must be cared for; a squad leader is as accountable for the changing of socks as he is for the cleaning of a machine gun. Men on alert must stay awake, no matter how exhausting the preceding hours have been. Radios have to be monitored, kept dry, and supplied with fresh batteries. Proper communication procedures must be maintained. Codes must not be compromised.

Positions must be constantly improved. The claymore mines have to be checked, camouflaged, and recamouflaged. Trenches have to be deepened. Firing positions must be made more lethal to the enemy. Artillery fires must be registered and reregistered. Grass adjacent to the wire must be kept cut. The ammunition bunker has to be kept dry. Soldiers must be rehearsed in all combat actions that may be expected of them. The functioning of the chain of command must be clearly understood by all the men. In combat, leaders are quickly attrited, and every man must, in his turn, be prepared to take over and continue the mission.

There was nothing new in my philosophy of command. It was the first order given to Roger's Rangers in the French and Indian War long before the establishment of the U.S. Army: "Don't forgit nothin'!" I did not plan to.

I adapted my lifestyle completely to fit in with my plans for the platoon. I slept in short spurts, more often during the day than at night. I continued to move with every third patrol. I checked each squad on the way out of the wire and counted each one on the way in: we weren't going to be infiltrated by the simplest of tricks, an enemy soldier at the tail end of a patrol returning in the dark. Nor were we going to lose a man through oversight: every soldier, every weapon, and every piece of equipment was accounted for after each patrol, and I was merciless with the squad leader who came up short on anything. And if there was an error in accounting, the platoon sergeant had better know of it first.

I checked positions at night, every night. I lay behind the machine guns of the men in the strong-points. I checked the frequency of the radio carried by the RTO. I ate my meals at irregular hours, sometimes alone, sometimes with a group of soldiers. I sat and listened to the men. I studied their manner of speech, their gait, the fact that they were left-handed or right-handed, how soundly they slept, how well they saw in the dark.

I listened to their stories, their hopes, their gripes. I tried not to speak about myself. Their concern about me was whether or not I could get them through their tour. They might want to tell me about their homes and their families, but they wanted me to listen, not talk. They did not want to know about my life away from Vietnam. I was an officer. In their eyes, that made me different. I was a part of this war. I was one of the ubiquitous "they." "They" drafted the soldier. "They" trained him. "They" ordered him to this godforsaken place. And "they" sent him out on terrifying missions to be maimed and killed. "They" did not have a life other than the army. "They" *were* the army.

So I listened, and I watched. These men were the

prime resource of the platoon; they would fulfill its missions. They would do their country's bidding. But they were men, first; they were not so many boots on parade. They were human; they had loves, fears, futures that they hoped to see. They made me wonder—was I coming to know them too well to make them do what they had to do? Or did I not know them well enough to ask them to do it? I listened to them, I watched them, and I thought about them.

I also thought about the enemy. It was somewhat unnerving to realize that there were people out there who meant to kill us. I knew they were watching us, studying every detail of our operations, looking for an opening. We had advantages, particularly in firepower and mobility, but they had advantages, too. They could see us. The villagers were their eyes and ears. They knew where the breaks in the wire were cut. They knew the number of soldiers I had, which weapons were functioning, and how new the leaders were. Binh Dinh province was a stronghold of the Viet Cong, and they were passing information to them. We could not just wish the enemy away. They were thinking. We had to think.

How many of them were there? How well did they know our operations? How timely was their information? What were they thinking? Where did they plan to come at us? Where would they put the booby traps? How many and what type of weapons did they have? Where would they position them? When would they strike?

What about their weaknesses? Surely they had weaknesses, just as we did. What were they? How could we capitalize on them? They had to eat; the food had to come from somewhere. They had to sleep; they had to let their guard down sometime. They had to gamble. They couldn't be strong everywhere; they had to take chances, a risk here for a gain there. We looked for them, stepped on booby traps, walked into ambushes.

They must have looked for us. They had to move, too. When did they move? Where did they move?

Know your enemy! To know your enemy is to defeat your enemy. To know your enemy is to kill your enemy. Kill your enemy? What kind of thought process was that? What madness. They were trying to kill us; we were trying to kill them. We were a group of average men—young men brought up in varying degrees of a central godly ethic. There might have been a few exceptions to that, but very few. The enemy were also young, also adherents of a humanistic faith in which killing was not the essence of life. Yet now we faced each other, obsessed with the idea of killing each other. There was no respite from it. Once a day I wrote a letter to my wife; it was a moment of sanity snatched from the madness of war. If anything, my thoughts of home reinforced my desire to stay alive and my determination to keep the enemy from killing me. They would not kill me; they would not kill my men. We would kill them first.

"War is the management of violence," claimed the contemporary social scientists and military strategists as we hacked our way through the struggle in Vietnam. For us, violence was killing; there was no management involved. People were either dead, or they were not. I could not "manage" my platoon up a hill. I had to lead them up there. I had a mission to accomplish, and I had men to keep alive, as many as I could.

I had to do more than keep them alive. I had to preserve their human dignity. I was making them kill, forcing them to commit the most uncivilized of acts, but at the same time I had to keep them civilized. That was my duty as their leader. They were good men, but they were facing death, and men facing death can forgive themselves many things. War gives the appearance of condoning almost everything, but men must live with their actions for a long time afterward. A leader has to help them understand that there are lines they must not cross. He is their link to normalcy, to order, to humanity. If the leader loses his own sense of propriety or shrinks from his duty, anything will be allowed. And anything can happen.

Some men in combat will commit war crimes, just as some men in combat will fail to take care of themselves. They will experiment with drugs, steal property, abuse women. When this happens it destroys the discipline of a unit, making it easier for others to follow suit.

War is, at its very core, the absence of order; and the absence of order leads very easily to the absence of morality, unless the leader can preserve each of them in its place. The leader has to set the standards for morality as clearly as he sets the standards for personal hygiene or weapons maintenance. He must allow no cutting of corners. A bottle of soda stolen from an old peasant woman leads gradually but directly to the rape of her daughter if the line is not drawn in the beginning.

Modern wars, particularly the Vietnam War, draw little distinction between battlefields and civilian communities. The callousness of war that infects soldiers was every bit as evident in the peasant population in the village where my platoon worked. The peasants were the families of the Viet Cong. They had been hardened by years of war. They resented the American presence, which threatened them. But they were men and women with the basic rights of human beings and the requisite needs for security and justice. The fact that some of them might kill you or your soldiers was no reason to hate them or to abuse them. This was war, this Vietnam involvement, and in war things tend to happen. But the commander was the link to order and civility, and he had to be humane. At the same time he had to be uncompromising to protect the lives of all. The job was not easy.

# CHAPTER 9

# A CAST OF CHARACTERS

Who were the sons that America sent to war? In vain I looked for the archetypal platoon of romantic fiction. The kid from Brooklyn wasn't there. (I fit the role better than any of the soldiers.) The incipient poet never made it. The rich mama's boy out to prove his manhood stayed home. As a cross section of America's youth, the platoon was a complete failure.

The military draft was never concerned with equity. Its sole purpose was to obtain the required numbers of men with sufficient mental and physical qualities to do the job. Since the pool of men from which to draw was much greater than the numbers needed, a natural selection process allowed the educated and the privileged to avoid the draft altogether. The selection process continued for the unfortunates drafted so that those with some education or particular skills would be diverted from combat service. Even among those who made it to Vietnam, the vast majority never saw combat. Only those without skill, without schooling, and without friends, or those who were obstinate in the face of ceaseless proselytizing against their obligation to serve, made it to the field.

And they knew it. I could see it in the faces of soldiers like Phil Nail, my RTO from Prospect Park, Pennsylvania. Phil claimed he was in Vietnam on an option, his alternative being a term in jail. He was an impish character who could always tell a good story, and while I didn't believe his personal story, he was so proud of it that I never revealed my doubts. What I did believe was that he saw no future in staying around Prospect Park. He may have been in trouble with the law; more likely it was trouble with a disgruntled father or a woman. Whatever it was, it had cost Nail twenty-two months in Vietnam and two Purple Hearts. Not that any of this embittered the man; his most obvious feature was a happy-go-lucky attitude. By his own admission, his disposition was the result of his skill at "getting over."

"Shit, L.T.," Nail would boast in his cocky Philadelphia accent, "I got it knocked."

"What do you mean you got it knocked? You're out here same as the rest of us, aren't you?" I would ask.

"Oh, but I'm the RTO. I ain't no goddamned rifleman anymore. I just carry the radio. None of the John Wayne shit for me." Nail was irrepressible. He was the platoon politician, dispenser of the sundry packet that arrived every week, and he would always slip the extra chewing gum or the better toothpaste to his "constituents." In his own eyes he was the man who beat the system. It was him against the career NCOs, the "lifers" as he called them. And as far as he knew, the "lifers" did not stand a chance.

But Phil Nail had the blood of the career NCO in his veins. The army was fast becoming his life, and if it was an army at war in which he happened to be weaned, so be it. Compared to the hundreds of thousands who avoided front-line combat, Phil Nail was not "getting over" at all. He was in it up to his neck and knew it, but he never showed that it bothered him.

Jim Barnes, from Asheville, North Carolina, knew it, too. Specialist Barnes came from a town renowned for its contribution to its country's military service in time of war. The men from the mountains around Asheville are descended from a hardy stock of frontiersmen who knew that you had to fight for what you believed in. Nonetheless, Barnes might have avoided Vietnam if fate had been less harsh to him. He was bright enough, and I imagine his grades in school had been good. He was enough of an athlete to have been awarded a scholarship. His independence of mind and his physical adroitness were soldierly qualities that could have served him well in more civilized endeavors. But Specialist Barnes, grenadier for the 1st Squad, stuttered to the point of incomprehensibility.

He was a powerfully built man whose large hands cradled his M-79 grenade launcher authoritatively. He moved with ease, his wide shoulders somehow passing through tight tangles of underbrush without disturbing their natural pattern. He knew his job well, followed orders wisely, and led by example. But when he spoke, his eyes rolled up, his mouth gaped open, and his throat strangled on every word.

His shame of his affliction was great. Somehow, he felt, he had disgraced his forebears. They were men to whom one listened. No one would listen to him. No one could wait for him to finish what he had to say. And so he did not go to college, or play ball, or get a job. He joined the army and was assigned to 2d Platoon, Bravo Company, 4th Battalion of the 503d Airborne Infantry Regiment. It was a mouthful, but he would never have to say it. Out here, the less he said, the safer it would be, and the more people would like him.

Corporal John Killigan, from Bakersfield, California, also knew there was a basic injustice in the way the war was being fought—and he relished every minute of it. At twenty-two years of age, he was already on his third tour of duty in Vietnam. Far and away, Killigan was the most combat-experienced soldier in the platoon, but although everyone respected him, no one considered him a friend. He had grown up in foster homes, and he traced his lineage to both Caucasian and Indian ancestors. He was the classic lone wolf. He took his meals by himself, and when he spoke, which was seldom, it was only one or two words in response to a question or a short expression of disdain. He did not address people by either their names or their titles. I was never "the lieutenant" or "sir." Our conversations were one-sided; he would listen to the orders and comply with them but never acknowledge them with a word or a nod. Instead, he would give a cold stare, his lips curling into a barely concealed sneer, and move off to do his job. Authority figures, particularly officers it seemed, were objects of a contempt he revealed only through his hard, unblinking eyes.

Despite Killigan's hostility toward military protocol, his disdain for new guys ("FNGs" he would mutter under his breath), and his aloofness from the rest of the men, he was the most respected member in the platoon. The reason was simple: he was the best soldier among us. He had the reflexes of a cat; he was a deadly shot and ferocious in a fight, and he never showed the slightest bit of concern for his own safety. He was the perennial point man, the man who leads the file on patrol, the soldier who will make first contact with the enemy, the one who first steps on the booby trap or first walks into the line of fire. His was the most dangerous job on patrol, yet he never complained. He was a complete stoic. If it rained, he refused to wipe the water from his brow. If a mission kept him awake for several days, he could be counted on to be the most alert man present. Killigan was an absolute infantryman. Every unit should have one like him.

If ever a man had the appearance of a killer, it was Killigan. In perhaps the longest conversation we ever held, Killigan told me how a group of college youths had tried to talk him out of entering the recruitment station. He was reenlisting, having been discharged after his second tour in Vietnam. "Don't let them draft you!" a young girl had pleaded. "Draft me?" was his derisive reply. "Lady, I'm asking for it. I want to go kill some of those bastards!"

He must have loved that story. It was the only one I ever heard him tell, and I believed every word of it. And so I made an assessment of Killigan, rated him as a fighter, and was glad to have him. How much more there was to him, I would find out in time.

The whole platoon was made up of men like Nail, Barnes, and Killigan. Each was different in personality and experience—from the hardened veteran to the fresh seventeen-year-old—but all were alike in that they were the few who kept falling through the sifting, discriminating screens of selection that deposited them at that lonely outpost in the midst of the enemy. There were so many ways to avoid ending up as a combat infantryman; there were so many of their countrymen who would never see an olive drab uniform or a drill sergeant, or the green hell of Vietnam. But each of these men seemed destined to end up there, as if it had been written in granite on the day of his birth.

They did not complain. They accepted their fate and looked to themselves, each other, and their leaders to get them through. It was ironic that their leaders were given so much trust. In many cases, the squad leaders had had less experience than the men they led. At that particular time, the army was drafting men from civilian life, putting them through a few weeks of basic and advanced individual training, and then sending some of them to a short course for a few months, after which they were promoted to NCO status in the rank of buck sergeant. Although the men selected were from the upper levels of their basic and advanced training groups, they still lacked the experience that takes a full-fledged NCO years to develop. But the army had no option. The Vietnam War was very expensive for the NCO corps. Many of the regulars had been lost, and the instant NCOs took their places. To their credit, many of those young men so abruptly removed from civilian life did a highly respectable job as squad leaders, and occasionally as platoon sergeants.

The platoon was not totally comprised of Americans. Among the young men, whose average age could not have been more than twenty-one years, was one "older" Vietnamese who was forty. Nguyen Nhan was a "Kit Carson" scout, a former Viet Cong who had defected and in return for amnesty had agreed to serve with the Americans. Nhan had been a Viet Cong for five years. He protested that it had not been his choice, that they had come to his village and forced him to serve. Whatever his original motivation for service, I suspect that he had been a good soldier. Nhan was nothing if not tough. At 5'8" he was tall for a Vietnamese, and there wasn't an ounce of fat on him; muscular arms and wrists indicated an earlier vocation as a woodcutter.

As far as I could tell, there were three things Nhan liked: cigarettes, women, and killing Viet Cong, probably in reverse order. Whatever he had been made to do as a Viet Cong, it had soured him toward their ideology. He knew that his days were numbered. He was already into what the Vietnamese considered middle age. He had received five Silver Stars from the U.S. Army, and had put forty-five notches in the stock of his M-16 for enemy he had personally killed. There was a price on his head throughout Binh Dinh province. He had moved his family into a neighboring province and visited them incognito. On the job, he took countless chances in pursuit of his quarry. One night as he lay in hiding, a Viet Cong walked by him. When Nhan's weapon misfired, he leaped into the kill zone of the ambush and beat the Viet Cong to death with the malfunctioning weapon. Nhan's aggressiveness was a personal liability that sooner or later would be his undoing. But until that happened, he would kill as many of his former comrades as he possibly could.

Nhan's replacement for the infrequent times he went on leave, usually to take his monthly pay back to his family, was another Kit Carson scout named Chong. Chong seemed to be the antithesis of Nhan. Where Nhan was deadly serious at his business, Chong, a little, pudgy fellow, always had a ready laugh and took life a bit easier. He was also less cautious than Nhan, electing to keep his family nearby so he could visit them frequently when he wasn't out in the field. His family lived in a small house in the village of Bong Son, just outside the gate of LZ English. Somehow, Chong felt their proximity to Brigade headquarters would protect them from the wrath of the Viet Cong, who were not kind to those who defected from their ranks.

Retribution came to Chong before my tour was over. One night as he lay sleeping with his wife, the Viet Cong payed him a visit. Chong himself was only subdued. His wife was killed as she lay beside him. His father and daughter also were killed. His mother's leg was hacked off, and although she lived for a little while, death came as a result of the emotional and physical shock. Chong returned to us to fight again, but his old amiability had left him. The war had claimed it.

Life for the Vietnamese was hard. For the United States, involvement in an undeclared war directly affected only a small percentage of our population and had no noticeable immediate effect on our economy. Not even our National Guard or Reserves were activated for this diversion in Southeast Asia. For the Vietnamese it was total war. No one was unaffected. I could see this in the village I was charged to secure.

The most noticeable thing about the village people was the absence of young men. They had all gone off to war on one side or the other. Those who were not killed would return occasionally for a family visit but only if they were serving with the Vietnamese government forces. The Viet Cong could not visit home so openly. However, since the Viet Cong generally worked in and around their own areas—at least in our portion of Vietnam—they probably had more contact with their families than the government soldiers. The large-scale absence of young men meant that the work of the village was done by the old people, the women, and the children. There were scores of children; there were obviously more visits being made by the menfolk than was apparent.

The most forlorn villagers were the young women. Approaching their womanhood in a time of war, they could only look forward to a few stolen moments with their men. Most would have short-lived marriages shattered by combat.

Every morning at seven the young women would come out of the village to make their way to the fields for the day's work. Even in black peasant pajamas, they were strikingly graceful and their features had the daintiness of a fine porcelain figurine. The American soldiers returning from their night patrol or ending the perimeter alert would watch longingly as the women passed by the wire only a few meters away.

I noticed one day that Specialist Barnes turned away when one particularly beautiful girl walked close by him as he was clearing a thicket of underbrush away from the wire. The girl's left arm was missing, her empty sleeve neatly folded and pinned to her shoulder.

"What's the matter, Barnes?" I asked.

In his painstakingly slow stutter, Barnes explained that the girl and her lover were among a group of armed Viet Cong who walked through one of our ambushes one night. The ambush was sprung. The boyfriend was killed, and the girl's arm was mangled by a bullet. The girl was evacuated by the Americans, but her arm could not be saved. Eventually, she returned to work her fields.

"What do you say to a girl whose arm you shot off?" Barnes asked me, his stutter clearing for a minute.

I could think of no reply.

The Vietnamese children were endearing. The boys were tough and swaggered when they walked. They would banter with the Americans in their Pidgin English, trying to sound insulting but betraying their affection for the men. This affection, however, did not prevent them from setting booby traps against us, and one day at the village well a young boy shot down a Vietnamese official we were protecting. There was nothing personal in these acts against us. The children were simply doing what their fathers and older brothers were doing. It was part of their lifestyle. But when an American was killed, the village children would line up as the survivors of the dead man's squad trooped by. They would count the returnees, note the missing man, and check the horizon for their "special friend" (and each child had a favorite); when he did not appear, they would turn away with tears in their eyes. This was a strange war.

Poignant as the children were, the most tragic villagers were the old people. They had known war all their lives, first with the Japanese, then with the French and Viet Minh, and finally with the Viet Cong, the Americans, the Government of South Vietnam, and the North Vietnamese. There was no hope now for a brighter future. There were only yesterdays of bloodshed and disrupted homes. Most of their male offspring were long gone, either dead or serving as soldiers, and if any of them came home, it was as invalids. All the old people could do was try to hold onto what little they had. While their female children offered the joy of companionship, the fatherless children they brought into the world only increased the burden on the elderly, who were already bent with age and heartbreak.

You couldn't blame the old ones for being callous, yet every now and then they would do something to remind you that they were like any other human beings anywhere in the world. An old woman, perhaps the mother of a Viet Cong, might look kindly on a freckle-faced American soldier. An old man, himself a veteran of combat on one side or another, might share a smoke with an NCO and talk about the way life used to be. These people were tough, but they had feelings.

Tran Van Dong, the middle-aged chief of Truong Lam, had that unique mixture of hardness and kindness that marked the village population. A small, solidly built man, he had only the slightest beginning of a paunch, despite his fifty-seven years. He had all the good-natured traits of a New York ward politician—the ready handshake (for the Americans, at least), the pat on the back, the off-color story, and the hearty laugh. He also had the instincts of a survivor. By his own account, Dong had been wounded no less than seven times: first as a soldier in his youth and then repeatedly as a government official in his maturity. Scars began at his left heel and wound up around his leg like a barber pole stripe. Deep puncture scars pocked his chest and back. A facial scar crossed his face from the point of his chin through the right corner of his mouth and up into his cheek. Stitch marks ridged the left side of his neck. His left eye was missing, but the right one gave off a glint of cold steel. In his belt he carried a cocked .45-caliber pistol. It seemed to me that only a madman would carry that weapon, known for its instability once primed for firing, in such a vital area. But to Dong the risk of accidental discharge was less than the risk of Viet Cong assassination. He would need every split second he could get if he had to defend himself.

None of us, neither the Americans, the Kit Carson scouts, the children, the women, nor the aged, knew why fate had thrown us together. We only knew that we were there and that we each had a part to play in a drama that was yet to be enacted. The enemy could not allow Truong Lam to stand as a testimony to the viability of the South Vietnamese government in the midst of a Viet Cong stronghold. We could not allow Truong Lam to fall. The people of Truong Lam waited to see which way the winds would blow. Together, we would resolve this dilemma in a contest that would allow no compromise, not for us, not for the enemy, and not for the people of Truong Lam.

# CHAPTER 10

# PRELUDE TO A FIGHT

Intelligence reports, those ominous forecasts of things to come (which no one knows whether to believe), began predicting a major enemy thrust in late September or early October. I was somewhat skeptical since I had received no major reinforcements or even replacements to cope with such a threat. (I was confident that the army would take the necessary steps to react to its own intelligence reports.) Nevertheless, I decided to waste no time improving my control as platoon leader.

My self-confidence was growing daily. The squads were reacting well to my orders, and I sensed a mutual trust between me and the squad leaders. Even the enemy was cooperating, staying close enough to keep us honest, but not pressing us to the point of a major test. So I had time to build our fighting strength.

My targets for improvement were discipline and tactics. The two are closely related. In the heat of battle there is no time for second-guessing the commander, and it is necessary for a soldier to develop an automatic response to an order. Such instantaneous obedience will overcome all fears, all confusion, all inclinations toward self-preservation. It is the result of unmitigated daily discipline in all things: from taking the daily malaria pill, to shaving each day, to attacking into the face of an automatic weapon.

The platoon was disciplined. Despite Lieutenant

Rolfe's inadequacies, the subordinate leaders had come forth to assert themselves. That, combined with the immediate dangers of combat, had preserved a disciplined unit. If the American press accounts were to be believed, the U.S. Army in the early 1970s was in a state of rebellion. That may have been so elsewhere, but I did not see it in my platoon. There was room for improvement, and I would work on that, but we were hardly a rebellious unit. We had, however, picked up some of the bad habits of the 1970s youth culture, among them the use of drugs.

One bright and sunny morning a resupply helicopter brought in a returning platoon veteran. Pfc James King of Louisville, Kentucky, had been wounded in action sometime before I arrived. An 82-millimeter mortar round had peeled off a large part of his back but had not penetrated deeply enough to incapacitate him for further service. It had taken several months for King to heal, and during that time he had been exposed to some of the vices rife in the noncombat areas of Vietnam.

A sullen-looking, short man, King made his way back to his old squad where he was told to take his gear and report to me. Grudgingly, he sauntered up to the command post and dropped his rucksack in a cloud of dust at my feet.

"Good morning, I'm Lieutenant McDonough," I greeted him.

"Yeah" was his only response.

I looked at his hard eyes. Beneath the bitterness I saw the fear. He had barely made it the last time, and now he was back to try his luck again. "Call me Lieutenant, I prefer that," I said.

"Sure, L.T." His mouth formed a sneer.

"Open your ruck," I ordered, ignoring his insolence. I sifted through his gear: a poncho liner, a few pairs of socks, some toilet articles, a girlie magazine. As I reached deeper into the ruck I felt something plastic and pulled up several packs of marijuana cigarettes.

"What's this crap?" I asked. He didn't answer.

"Look, soldier, you've been goofing off in the rear for some time now," I said. "What you did back there, leave back there. Up here I want you alert. You just made a bad mistake. One more like that, and you'll be in big trouble.

"Give me your matches," I ordered.

Scowling, he handed me a book of matches. I soaked his marijuana in mosquito repellent, a good combustible, and set it afire. His eyes darkened as the stench rose from the smokey pile.

"Get back to your squad. We move out on patrol in an hour." I made a mental note to keep my eye on him.

A short time later, I walked over to check the squad out. I had increased the weaponry carried by the individual patrols, and I wanted to inspect for compliance. An M-60 machine gun with a double load of ammunition, twelve hundred rounds, would go on this patrol. Additionally, each man, including me, would carry a LAW. Although there were no enemy tanks in the area, the one-shot, disposable antitank weapon was highly effective in breaking up an enemy ambush. While it normally did not hit anything, it made such a terrible noise that it broke the enemy's will to stay in place.

King was carrying an M-79 grenade launcher as his weapon. I checked him out and moved up the line to inspect the other soldiers. Suddenly there was a hollow-sounding explosion and a whistling past my ear, followed by another explosion a second later about one hundred-fifty meters out in the bushes. I spun around to see King with a sneer on his face.

"Sorry, L.T.," the words hissed from his mouth. "I dropped my weapon."

The grenade launcher dangled from his right hand, a waft of smoke curling up from the barrel. It was clear he had fired the 40-millimeter round at me. At that range he could not have missed, so he must have meant it as a warning. He was telling me he did not like my attitude.

I was scared, but I was angry, too. King had not only threatened my life, but my authority as well. A few weeks earlier I might have been overcome by the situation, but since then I had developed the thick skin necessary for survival in Vietnam. With murder in my eyes I looked into King's face. Slowly, deliberately, I walked up to him, saying nothing until I was close enough to touch him. I had made no threatening gesture. Suddenly, when I was close enough to smell his breath, I flicked my M-16 to the fire position and placed the muzzle of the weapon in the cavity of the underside of his chin. He went up to his toes as I increased the pressure of the rifle barrel, lifting up against the bottom of his head.

The sneer was now on my face as I raised my voice so everyone could hear: "You son of a bitch." The eyes of everyone in the platoon were riveted on us. "Drop your weapon again, and you'd better pray to God it hits me square in the back. Because if it doesn't, you bastard, I'll blow your brains to kingdom come!"

Not a man stirred. My finger touched the trigger gingerly and King's eyes widened. The sullen look was gone from his face and beads of sweat formed on his forehead. Slowly I rotated him as he stretched to keep his toes touching the ground. He, as well as the others, knew that the slightest twitch would send a spray of bullets up through his face and out his head. For thirty seconds I let him hang suspended in terror. My rage had passed, but I was committed to play the scene out to its conclusion. Then, slowly, I lowered him off the barrel and flicked the weapon back to safe.

"All right. Let's go." I tried to sound calm.

As I walked away I awaited the blast that would tear my head off. I was betting that his bravado was only a bluff, that he really didn't have the nerve to kill me, but the choice was his. To turn back, to watch him, would ruin my act. Now I was the one who was sweating. But I could not flinch, and I did not. I gave the order to move out, and we left. King took his position in line and went through the wire with us. I had won.

I was indebted to King. He had given me a clear chance to establish my authority over the platoon once and for all, and from that point on I would never fear any of my own men. The experience gave me the self-confidence to take the platoon through whatever might come. My solution might not have earned the approval of the infantry school at Fort Benning, Georgia, but it was the best one I could think of at the time. How close King had come to pulling the trigger I will never know, but there was no time to dwell on it. I had to focus on the enemy.

The intelligence predictions of a major enemy attack in our area were becoming more assertive. The usual caveats, the built-in margins for error that normally appear in such reports, were being omitted. Whoever was writing them was sure the enemy was going to strike.

But if that were so, why wasn't I receiving more men? My platoon strength was diminishing as booby trap casualties outnumbered replacements. Although a Vietnamese RF platoon had recently arrived at the village, it was difficult to count them as increased combat strength. The reputation of the RF, a sort of Vietnamese National Guard, was poor. As in all military units, leadership was vital to effectiveness, and leadership in the

RF in general was not good. The lieutenant who arrived
with the platoon and immediately set up his hammock
beside the village well did not seem to be an exception.
I tried to instill our own aggressive tactics in him, but I
could not penetrate beyond the superficial handshakes
and smiles. His platoon had not come to fight, but to
avoid as much of the war as possible. While we pa-
trolled the countryside, they rested in the shade of the
village.

I wondered what the villagers thought of them. For
that matter, I wondered what the villagers thought of
us. Perhaps they did not think about us at all, except
when we directly affected their lives. They certainly had
enough of their own concerns.

At the edge of the village of Truong Lam lived an
old woman named Miss Ky, a kindly, grandmotherly
person who had taken in approximately fifteen children
whose parents had been scattered by the war. She was
by nature a pleasant person, and the necessities of car-
ing for so many young lives inclined her toward a
friendly relationship with the Americans. Each day Miss
Ky would hail us with a hearty greeting as she approached to barter some of her ample supply of rice,
contributed by the efforts of her "children" and the village people, for our C rations. Her friendly face was
welcome. We did take the precautionary step of opening
each can before we gave it up, lest the C rations make
their way to the Viet Cong, giving them handy, portable
food. But the transaction, for the most part, was made
in good faith. We enjoyed the rice, which we saturated
with our army-issued hot sauce (a curious supply item
of the U.S. Army in Vietnam). At the same time, Miss
Ky procured some of the nutrition she needed for the
children. It was a reasonable and understandable eco-
nomic relationship, but one that would cost the poor
old woman dearly.

Sergeant James Robinson, the hefty replacement for the wounded Sergeant Bradshaw, pushed his squad out to the southwest one bright morning the first week in October. Robinson was having a hard time measuring up to his responsibilities. A great bulk of a man from rural Alabama, his size had earned him a job as a cadre member of the U.S. Airborne School at Fort Benning, where they pick men for their imposing appearance. But the job of rifle squad leader in Vietnam was a little more than Robinson could handle, and for that reason I had assigned Specialist Barnes to the squad. Although Barnes had trouble talking, he could show Robinson the right way to do things.

It was Barnes who passed Sergeant Robinson the radio headset that morning as they came upon the grisly scene six hundred meters from the platoon base.

"Pilot Twister Two-One, this is Pilot Twister Five-Two, over," came Robinson's voice over the radio.

"This is Two-One Alpha, over," answered Phil Nail, sitting dutifully by his radio.

"This is Five-Two. Tell Two-One he'd better come quick. We've got a body lying across the trail to our front, over." Robinson's voice sounded shaky.

I told Nail to get the location in code, and yelled to Sergeant Donne to prepare his squad to move out. Then I instructed Robinson to leave the body alone until I got there. (It was not uncommon for the enemy to booby-trap the dead.) Thirty minutes later I arrived at the scene.

Barnes had already procured a long limb and was poking at the corpse to find out if it was mined. The body was clear, and the two of us moved up to make a closer inspection. I was becoming fairly accustomed to viewing the dead, but this cadaver was particularly grotesque. It was the old woman who had cared for the children. Both her breasts had been half-severed from her body, a deliberate cut made on the underside of each. Each palm and the sole of each foot had been shot through with a small-caliber round. The killing wound, which no doubt had followed the earlier torturous wounds, was a blast from a weapon evidently placed inside her mouth and directed out the back of her head. Her eyes were open, transfixed in terror. Jabbed into her belly on the end of a straightened safety pin was a note. Nhan, the Kit Carson scout, translated it for me:

"Tuan Cao Ky has been found guilty by the People's Court of aiding the American imperialists in their suppression of the Vietnamese people. As an enemy of the people, she has been made to pay for her crimes. This is the justice that will be brought to all who consort with the Americans and aid them in the villainous suppression of our land."

We dragged the body to the side of the trail, leaving it for burial by those who would be sympathetic to her plight. As we moved back into the village, we passed five of the younger children the woman had kept. Their faces were downcast.

The enemy was out there. They had left their calling card that morning, as they had left it before. There would be no recriminations of war crimes for this particular act. Nor would the world hear of it. It was not newsworthy, it was commonplace. But we in the platoon knew of it, and it grieved us. We had failed to protect Miss Ky. The enemy had won a victory and left us even more isolated. I stepped up our operations.

# CHAPTER 11

# BATTLE

Loneliness had filled the vacuum created by my deliberate aloofness from the platoon. Although I was getting to know the men—their fears, the lives they had left behind, their hopes for the future—I kept my own emotions to myself. I believed that to be the only proper course. I was the final authority in that piece of the world, the arbiter of right and wrong, life and death. I was afraid to put a human face on that authority.

And so I remained a part of my platoon, yet apart from my men. They might turn to me, but I turned to no one. Except for the letters to and from my wife, my feelings remained inside. I remembered the camaradarie of West Point and missed it sorely.

By October 9 the platoon strength had dwindled to eighteen soldiers, myself, and Nhan, the scout. Two of the squads were down to five men each, half their normal size, and the third was down to six. Platoon Sergeant Hernandez, Nhan, Nail, and I comprised the platoon headquarters.

The first patrol for the evening of October 9 pushed off around 1630. Six men, one a machine gunner, moved off to the northwest, going out about twenty-five hundred meters. By 1830 they had set up an ambush position, but as soon as darkness fell, around 1900, they shifted five hundred meters to the south. It was pretty clear to us by that time that Viet Cong sympathizers among the peasants were fixing our ambush locations before dark, and through a series of predetermined signals, were passing our location on to the enemy. Hoping to confound enemy intelligence, it became our policy to shift location after the initial halt.

At 2045 the first ambush patrol started sweeping back in from the north and was counted in through the wire around 2115. Fifteen minutes later the second patrol of the night pushed out. I considered joining that one, but since we were in a period of heightened alert, I elected instead to stay inside the platoon perimeter where I could direct the majority of the platoon. Already, by 2130, the RF platoon in the village was bedding down for the night.

At 2200 I dozed off in the shallow trench dug in the middle of the platoon perimeter. I had kept all three machine guns back, one mounted at each strong-point on the tips of the perimeter triangle. The RTO, Phil Nail, the happy-go-lucky kid from Pennsylvania, was sleeping on an air mattress about six feet from my slit trench. Platoon Sergeant Hernandez had moved inside his sandbagged bunker. By right of rank I would have had the bunker for my own quarters had I wanted it, but I had passed it up for a number of reasons. It was too plush in comparison to what the men had; it was too easy to get trapped inside of it in a firefight and thus be unable to control the platoon; and it was no doubt noted and duly marked by the enemy as a convenient point of reference. (I did not want to make myself an easy target.)

Around 2400 I awoke and nudged Nail to join me with his radio as I checked the perimeter. The men were on a one-third alert inside the wire, and since only eleven men (excluding the platoon CP) were there at that particular time, that meant only four people were awake. It was enough for our small perimeter.

At half past midnight I began to get a bad feeling

about the squad out on ambush. Although we had been in radio contact, and they were only seven hundred meters away, I wanted to bring them in to consolidate my strength. The order to return was passed by radio, and by 0105 they were moving in through the wire. I debriefed the squad leader, who had the normal jitters after a night operation. He reported nothing unusual out in the darkness.

Phil Nail and I moved back to our position at the center of the perimeter. My feet were sore from days and days of wearing boots, and I pulled them off to stretch my toes and air them out. Phil told me he was wide awake now and asked if he could go and talk to his buddy who had just come in from patrol. As that was a distance of only twenty meters, I gave him the okay, but warned him not to leave his radio alone for a moment and to get back to me in a flash should anything happen. "Sure, lieutenant," Nail replied as he moved away.

Some of the men were still readjusting themselves into position as I stretched out in my trench. My thoughts were drifting back to my wife and I wondered what she might be doing while I was lying there. In the soft stillness of the night I felt fairly relaxed. I would be home someday. I only needed to allow the time to pass.

A hollow-sounding plop disturbed the gentleness of the night. Then three or four more plops followed close on the heels of the first and, only a second later, ten or fifteen more. I had been in combat long enough to recognize the sound of a 40-millimeter round leaving the tube of an M-79 grenade launcher. We had about ten seconds before the explosion of shells would rake our positions.

I rolled over on my stomach and shouted a warning to the platoon: "Incoming!"

Those asleep rolled out and moved toward their

weapons. The men on alert dashed for the trenchline. The second wave of 40-millimeter shells left their deceptively quiet launchers just before the first wave of rounds landed with a barrage-type effect inside the perimeter. Ear-shattering explosions burst right on top of us. There would be no need for the enemy to adjust the mortar-like deluge; they were right on target. I saw the flash of one burst light up the feet of one of my soldiers. It is suicidal to run in a barrage, and I yelled for everyone to get down. I should have saved my breath. My voice was drowned out in the explosions. The night was bright with bursting shrapnel and flashing gunpowder. Then came the chatter of automatic weapons fire. The enemy was coming at us in force. I scrambled to put my boots on.

A high-pitched scream rose above the din of the battle. One of my men had been hit a few meters off to my left on the eastern perimeter of the wire. A shard of shrapnel had penetrated deep into his thigh and ruptured a nerve, causing excruciating pain. He howled an unbroken stream of curses intermixed with plaintive appeals to God, his mother, and anyone else he could think of at the moment. I winced and gritted my teeth. I would have to get to him later.

The first thing I needed was my radio. I called out to Nail to get over to me quickly, but there was no response above the racket of gunfire and exploding shells. I made an estimate on the location and range of the enemy. They were close, and spread out in such a way as to gain converging fire across our position. A force was located immediately to our southeast, actually within the village of Truong Lam. Another force was due south, raking our position with at least one machine gun and several automatic weapons. From the southeast and from the west came a heavy volume of fire and the majority of the M-79 rounds. All enemy elements were within two hundred fifty meters of us, and the force in the village was only some sixty meters away. Again I called for Nail, and again I got no answer.

The RF platoon had been caught completely unprepared. The enemy was right among them, and they were caught in a torrid crossfire as we opened up in return. I could hear the bullets ripping through the barbed wire, making a frightening twanging noise. Spontaneously, the RF platoon made a dash through the upright steel poles holding the wire in place. I yelled at Donne's squad guarding the south wire to hold fire, and we let them come through. Most of them seemed all right, although they carried in some wounded. They immediately sought cover, assuming a posture that indicated I could not expect much further help from them.

Again I yelled for Nail and the all-essential radio. We were in for a tough fight, and the radio was our link to all outside support. I had to have it.

"Nail, you SOB," I shouted, "get your ass over here!"

In the darkness immediately to my front I heard a soft cry: "I can't make it."

Nail was hit, and the realization gave me the impetus to move. I crawled to where his plaintive response seemed to originate. He lay sprawled on his side, his radio firmly strapped to his back. Blood was spurting from his right leg and flowing from his mouth. I felt sick. Nail was the man closest to me in the platoon. Since my return, we had barely been apart, and his light banter always brightened my inherently serious outlook. I wanted to stop the action. The battle had gone too far. Not Nail! I wanted to stop his bleeding. I wanted to get him out of there. I wanted to save him. But there was no time. Yelling for the medic, Lawrence, to come over from Donne's squad, I removed Nail's radio and put it on my back. Then I crawled up to the southernmost machine gun, leaving Nail behind me.

I pointed out to the machine gunner where I wanted him to place his fire as I called over the radio to the company command post. An RTO returned my call, but to my dismay he told me the company commander was not there. He had returned earlier in the day to the battalion headquarters at LZ North English. I was more alone than I thought. I told the RTO to reach the battalion command net and have them come up on my frequency.

Two more of my men let out a yell off to the left as a 40-millimeter shell landed between them in the trench. I now had fourteen Americans left and a Kit Carson scout. The fight was less than ten minutes old. I moved over to the wounded men, took up their position, and began to return fire with my own M-16.

The platoon sergeant had made it out of his sandbagged sleeping position and crawled to the north side of the perimeter. We were not under fire there, except for the rounds grazing across the center of the perimeter from the south and the east. The sergeant called for the machine gun from the position there to come across to the southern perimeter. That done, we began to put some heat on the enemy along the south and the southeast. I yelled for three riflemen from the northern trenchline to make it over to my position, where we were distinctly short of men. I had to move over to the western side, as we were still being raked there by close-in automatic fire.

When the three riflemen arrived, I made a dash across the center of the platoon position, but machine gun fire ripping across the ground to my front forced me to go down. I waited a second and dashed again. A wounded Vietnamese soldier from the RF platoon was sprawled in my path, and before I could shift my momentum I bounced over him. He winced and I could see blood flowing in a heavy stream from his side. He cursed at me, and I knew in an instant he was dying.

Unable to go any farther in the face of the fire, I crawled to a mound of dirt and tried once again to raise some help with the radio. This time the company commander's voice came over the net. He sounded groggy from sleep and kept insisting that I describe to him what was happening. At one point he asked for a description of the uniform the enemy was wearing. The conversation was getting me nowhere so I cut it short by insisting that I had to get back to the action.

My timing was good. At that moment the first rush was made by the enemy. Twenty to thirty Viet Cong appeared, coming at the south wire at a dead run. I shouted for my men to shift their fire on them. There was no need for my words. My men were responding well. We were getting off a hand-held flare every thirty seconds, which illuminated the rushing enemy very clearly. The two machine guns on that portion of our perimeter barked out a welcome in neat six-round bursts. Several of the enemy fell. Their first rush was stopped in its tracks.

The radio crackled and I answered a call from the battalion S-3, Major Buckworth, the operations officer. His line of questioning was much more direct than the company commander, who had been wasting my time. When he asked me what I needed, I told him to send up some Cobra helicopter gunships as well as some indirect fire for illumination, as we would soon be out of hand-held flares. The enemy would have a distinct advantage in full darkness. I explained that under indirect fire we could take the attackers with our own M-79s, as they were well within the weapons' four-hundred-meter range.

Our business done, Major Buckworth broke off the

conversation, leaving me free to direct the fight. Within a few minutes, illumination rounds from the battalion tubes began popping overhead.

I renewed my movement to the western side of the perimeter. I knew the enemy would make a move from there any minute, and I wanted to greet them when they came. It was becoming increasingly clear that the machine gun was going to be the key weapon in the initial stage of the fight. I made it up to the machine gunner, after stopping a few more times along the way to take cover from the incoming rounds. The gunner was doing fine, not at all intimidated by the enemy fire. He was looking for some guidance as to where to work his gun. Ordinarily that was the job of the squad leader, but he had been put out of action with some shrapnel through his upper torso and neck. The senior man left in the squad was an E-5 buck sergeant, so I put him in charge and told him where I thought the enemy rush would come from. Just then the artillery flares started coming in and we could see about forty figures moving around out there. The squad reacted magnificently, sending out a stream of molten steel. The enemy stopped advancing. For the first time, I felt we could hold.

On the southern end of the perimeter another American soldier took a hit, a round through the shoulder. Our only medic was having a busy night of it. I now had thirteen Americans left in the action.

The platoon sergeant was doing his job getting the ammunition out. Each man had an ample supply to begin the action, but we were in for a long fight and the key to our holding would be a continued heavy volume of fire. I was doing what I could to direct that fire in a controlled fashion, but in the heat of battle excessive amounts of ammunition are expended despite all efforts at control. The best I could do was to moderate the fire, trying to put it in when and where I thought it would do the most good. I did this by firing tracer rounds in the direction I wanted a particular sector to focus on. As a precaution I had loaded my magazines with every fifth round as a tracer. I also had set aside one full magazine with nothing but tracer, which I would use to signal the platoon's final protective fire, a preplanned last stand at a maximum rate of fire. The tracer bullet burned a red line clearly distinguishable in the darkness, pointing to the intended target. The Communist weapons had tracers too, a bright green. In the dark, the deadly colors crossed each other, brilliant fingers of death searching out intended victims.

The night was a carnival of sound and color: the whistling, flickering flares; the bright explosives; the screaming wounded; cries for help, cries for more fire, and cries for ammunition; machine guns beating out a deafening staccato; the wire snapping under the harsh bite of lead bullets.

The platoon medic, Sp4c. Brad Lawrence, the son of an active-duty army colonel, was making his way toward the rifleman hit in the shoulder. Lawrence was a good medic but a rebellious soldier, caught between his own antiwar sentiments and his father's wishes that he serve in the military. As a compromise he volunteered to be a medic, by definition a noncombatant. I liked Lawrence, but his permanently dilated pupils made me suspect that he was probably the platoon's biggest drug user.

But that night he was seeing clearly. From the southeast a woman came running toward the break in the wire. She was carrying a bulky object in her arms, but in the flickering light of the flares it was impossible to identify it.

"Don't fire!" Lawrence barked.

I was not sure I agreed. If it was a satchel charge the woman was carrying she would be able to fling it in at us in another few steps. The explosion would rip that part of the perimeter wide open, allowing the enemy to rush through unimpeded. On the other hand, if the woman was seeking help it would be a tragedy to cut her down.

As I hesitated, the heavy beat of enemy rounds forced her down. Lawrence made a dash for the wire, got ten steps, and then went into a low crawl. Inching his way along, he made it to a break in the wire and came up to the woman. In her arms was her seven-year-old daughter. The little girl had taken a round clean through the chest; a lung was collapsed, and she was bleeding heavily. Her mother was trying to make it to us to save the child.

Lawrence placed his body between the enemy fire and the mother and child and proceeded to treat the wound. Sucking chest wounds are difficult to stabilize under the best of conditions. Raising himself up on one knee, Lawrence sealed off the two holes, front and back, with plastic from the dressings he carried. He was trying to get the child's chest cavity properly pressurized so she could breathe. He worked quickly as Specialist Barnes came out to cover him. In a few minutes the two men dragged the mother and child inside the wire.

As the four of them entered the perimeter, the enemy came at the southeast corner in a rush, trying to follow them. Once more, the interlocking machine gun fire forced the attackers back. The fighting was stabilizing. Although M-79 grenades continued to fall among us, we minimized their threat by keeping low. Discounting the RF platoon, which had made no move to help us, we were still badly outnumbered. But time was on our side. Roughly one-third of my men were hurt, but I had plenty of ammunition, and support was on the way. If I could keep the enemy from massing for a concentrated assault, we would have a good chance of holding them off.

As if on cue, I heard the *whump-whump-whump* of

helicopters approaching: a pair of Cobra gunships, sleek and heavily armed, spewing out an intense volume of fire from multibarreled machine guns and launching high-explosive rockets. Help had arrived!

The words of the gunship team leader broke in over the air waves, the vibrations of his helicopter causing his voice to quiver. In the chatty but authoritative tone peculiar to pilots, he told me he was about to rain trouble on the enemy but needed my help. Although he had the village in sight, he couldn't differentiate friend from foe. From his perspective, the antagonists were locked in very close combat. Though the southern edge of the village had caught fire, lighting the target area, and the interlocking tracers revealed the location of the antagonists to some degree, the pilot still wasn't sure where to aim his machine guns.

For a moment I was mesmerized by the offer of help. It was as if the responsibility for the battle had just been lifted from my shoulders. The voice reaching me from above sounded so assured, so much in charge. In my mind, a senior officer sat in the lead cockpit ready to save the lieutenant and his platoon from the encroaching enemy. I saw him as a major. Majors talked that way.

"I can see some movement by the fire in the village," he said. "I'll bring my fire there, over." It was not a question; it was a statement of fact.

I crouched for a moment in silence as the two gunships lined up for their strafing run. In a few seconds thousands of rounds would tear into the village, ripping through the grass huts, slaughtering the penned livestock, and tearing the inhabitants apart. I had only to sit there and let it happen. In a few seconds it would be done. The helicopters swooped into their dive.

"Negative, negative!" I cried out. "Hold your fire!"

The choice was mine, not the pilot's. It did not matter who he was. I was the senior ground commander. I was the one responsible for the situation there. Quiet acceptance of the slaughter of the villagers would not relieve me of the moral responsibility for their death. Even though the enemy was firing on us from the village, even though a third of my men had fallen in the action, I could not kill a community of innocent people in order to destroy the enemy hiding amongst them.

"Bring your fire in to the south and west, about seventy-five meters," I ordered. "I will put in tracer on the position. Authenticate before you fire." Once more I was fully accepting my responsibility, but I shivered at the realization of what I had almost allowed.

The helicopters swooped in, picked out my targets, and expended their ordnance. There was an immediate hush as the enemy dove for cover. My men were visibly cheered.

The overwhelming advantage of firepower and mobility available to U.S. forces in Vietnam was impressive. We could concentrate power on any enemy who chose to stay and fight it out. If an American unit could survive the first minutes of fighting, normally it could survive the battle. Consequently, the enemy attacking us was forced to face an unpleasant but simple decision: stay and die, or break contact. It was about ten minutes later when our armored relief element came into view, and until that time the enemy continued to pour lead in on us. But already I had begun to shift my tactics to the offensive. I wanted to take a squad and link up with the tanks and armored personnel carriers. Donne's squad had been badly chewed up in the fight. Sergeant James, the eager youngster from Valdosta, Georgia, had been hit. Robinson had been pretty scarce during the fighting, so I figured it was his turn to take chances. I took his squad with me, leaving my platoon sergeant to organize the evacuation of the wounded and the continued security of the perimeter.

I raised the cavalry platoon over the radio, telling them we would join them and pursue the enemy as they tried to break away, probably to the south. We exited through the northern part of the wire, and I kept up a constant chatter as we closed with our relief force. I didn't want to risk getting shot at by big iron monsters. Within a few minutes we linked up. I found the platoon leader's tank and climbed up. The leader was a West Point classmate, Larry O'Brien, and although I had not known him at the Academy, I couldn't have been happier to see him.

The rifle squad and I felt invincible. Something about all that steel made us feel secure, even though we were perched on top of it. Like so many charioteers, we led the armored platoon after the enemy, who were frantically breaking away into the darkness. Larry opened up with his machine gun and then let fly from his main gun a "beehive" round, a shell filled with hundreds of little darts that cut a giant scythelike swath in its path. The enemy, however, was getting away. In that terrain, man was much faster than machine.

In a final twist of fate, one of the tanks collapsed a hidden underground bunker into which two of the enemy had crawled. The men were crushed horribly by the multiton monster. Beyond that, the killing was over for the night. I took my small force of five and made one final dismounted sweep of the area as the armored vehicles covered us. After that we moved back to the perimeter. It was five o'clock in the morning. We had been fighting for four hours. I felt drained. I seemed to have no emotional reaction to the night of battle. My greatest need, as the sun rose over the horizon and sent its welcome rays in our direction, was to relieve myself.

There was no time to go through the niceties of digging a cathole, so I did it in an empty sandbag.

I went about the business of reconsolidating my defenses and checking the wounded who had not yet been evacuated. I glanced at the dead as they were collected. The dead look so forlorn. A corpse immediately takes on an appearance of loosely packed earth piled into oversized clothes. It was a dismal scene, the line of bodies growing at the edge of the smoking huts in the southern extreme of the village. As acrid smoke rose, it spread the putrid smell of death over the remnants of my platoon. I tried to remain objective as I took a tally of the night's fight.

None of my men was dead. Two were badly wounded but had a better-than-even chance of pulling through. Nail, who had looked a mess when I saw him in the dark, had bled heavily from his leg but would pull through and return a few weeks later. His bloody mouth was the result of a piece of shrapnel that had torn into his gums and knocked out a tooth. From his point of view, he had "gotten over" again. We evacuated the little girl with the hole in her chest. She never returned, dying in the hospital. The Vietnamese soldier I had stumbled over was dead by dawn. Sergeant James, a bullet high in his shoulder and shrapnel up and down his left side, would return a few days before Nail. Two Vietnamese women from the village were among the bodies; each had been shot at close range in the base of the skull. It was my guess that the Viet Cong had executed them during the fight, but during the ensuing days propaganda leaflets would be found accusing the Americans of murder. Miraculously, the two women and the girl were the only villagers killed. The rest of the bodies were Viet Cong. My inspection done, I returned to my command post.

Larry O'Brien came over to join me for breakfast.

As we heated up two cans of water for coffee, we quickly agreed to put his platoon under my operational control. The battle had been Larry's first action, and he was elated. I congratulated him on his outstanding rescue of us poor infantrymen. I was happy to have another officer to talk to after such a long period of keeping myself aloof from the platoon. Despite the macabre scene forming in the village below, I felt pleased. It was as if a long-lost brother had appeared; we sat and ate our breakfast, warmed over our GI heat tabs, broad smiles on both our faces.

The morning haze was burning off the ground. The night had been grim, but dawn had brought me a friend. Soon we would begin patrolling again, but for the moment I would share my breakfast and talk.

# CHAPTER 12

# AFTERMATH

Killigan was point man on the first patrol out the morning after the fight. All night he had worked the machine gun from the southern tip of the platoon triangle, his steady hand holding the enemy rushes at bay. Early in the fight, the attackers had recognized Killigan's prowess and tried their best to put him out of action. The sandbags surrounding his position were torn and pocked from the bullets and shrapnel aimed at his early retirement. He had not flinched throughout the night. And now he took up the point with the alertness of a well-rested cat. The man seemed indestructible.

The rest of us were tired, however, and I hastened the patrol. How beautifully serene the morning was, the peaceful scene betrayed only by the smell of death that hung on the air. There were no signs of the enemy, and after two hours of searching I was confident that they had cleared out of the area. I turned back to face the details that come in the wake of battle.

My emotions were breaking through the fatigue that had numbed them, and my mood shifted dramatically from one extreme to another. At the moment I felt self-confident. I had come through a fight in which the initial odds, at least, were heavily against us. As I reviewed the bidding, it seemed that the early decisions had been sound. The sixth sense that had caused me to move in the one patrol ahead of schedule had been fortuitous.

Had the enemy struck while my meager forces were split, they might have overwhelmed one or both elements piecemeal. Controlling the separated elements also would have been almost impossible, and the subsequent coordination of outside support such as the air strike and the armored platoon would have been too hazardous had we even survived long enough to receive their help. My self-confidence was born of my awareness that luck had been on our side, as well as my own assessment that I had done most of the fighting correctly. Above all, I had not panicked, and I never lost control of the action. My sense of accomplishment was exhilarating.

On the other hand, I knew that the night's battle was merely one of many challenges yet to come. Although I had come through one fight, I would surely face many more. Would my luck hold out? In the long run, the odds were bound to right themselves.

My eyes returned to the bodies lying so neatly in line. Why did we line them up, anyway? Was it a penchant for neatness, an attempt to bring some orderliness to the disorder of death? It was so absurd. I remembered reading somewhere that in World War II the Germans had lined up the bodies of American prisoners they had massacred. Disorder and order, barbarity and civility—ironic juxtapositions in the affairs of men.

My elation was reduced to a sense of insignificance by the cold, brown look of the corpses sprawled in the bright sunlight. A few hours ago each one had been a dynamo of human spirit, hope, and ambition. Now they were still, their motion frozen at the last instant of life, as if making a mockery of the final effort. They had become meaningless clumps of earth, forever inanimate, no more significant than the rocks lying to their left and right. How fickle those human ambitions now seemed, how pointless those concerns.

And just as the bodies had become a part of the earth on which they rested, so I had passed during the battle from being in the war to being a part of the war. I was no longer an alien in a strange environment. I could no longer draw a distinction between the war and my presence in it. The preceding weeks had prepared me, but the battle itself had caused the final metamorphosis. The war had become a part of me, and I a part of it. And though my recognition of that fact was unnerving, I knew that probably within my transition lay the seeds of my ultimate survival.

My thoughts were broken by the sound of helicopters. I was about to be swamped by a deluge of official visitors to the scene of the battle for Truong Lam. Throughout the war in Vietnam, American generals, colonels, sergeant-majors, and other assorted dignitaries liked to arrive as soon as possible after the action (which, to my cynical mind, meant as soon as it was safe). That was their way of becoming a part of the action, of reassuring themselves that they had done their bit for the troops.

But perhaps I was too hard on them. They also wanted to show the soldiers that they cared. In fairness, the visits were not without personal risk. The enemy might not be far away. He might come back, eager to take advantage of a prime target. Moreover, the visitors were essential to the decision-making process that would determine the future of my platoon. The congratulatory comments on having come through the night, clearly intended to boost morale, did reassure the remaining defenders, and the advice the commanders gave on readjusting positions to compensate for noted vulnerabilities was helpful.

Even the general visited us that morning. How dignified he looked. He made me feel self-conscious because I hadn't even cleaned up after the fight. Perhaps I shouldn't have taken time to share my breakfast with Larry O'Brien. Better to have shaved and washed, inspected my men, and moved on to my duties. How slovenly of me.

But the general did not seem to notice. He walked the perimeter with me as I explained the course of the battle. He noted how few men I had at the beginning of the fight and how many fewer remained in the aftermath.

"I had better send you some men quickly, hadn't I, lieutenant?"

"Yes, sir." I tried to sound emphatic, but in truth I was wishing he had thought of that before the battle, especially since the intelligence reports had been so certain we would be attacked. But I was not about to deny our need for reinforcements now. My platoon barely amounted to a large squad.

As the general moved toward his waiting helicopter, he turned to say good-bye. Smartly I stood at attention in the downdraft of the rotating helicopter blades, straining to hear his words above the noise. "By the way, Lieutenant McDonough, I was listening on the radio when you diverted the gunships from hitting the village. That would have been a real mess. Good call."

"Thank you, sir."

He didn't hear me. He had turned and bounded aboard the helicopter, and I stood alone in the rushing wind. I stifled an urge to call after him, "Why didn't you say something last night?" But that would have been insubordinate. And perhaps he was right. The call was mine to make, not his. I was the commander on the ground, the man in the arena. I saluted the helicopter as it sped up and away, and turned back to the platoon.

One official who failed to visit on that day was the company commander. I noticed his absence with disgust. He had been away from the field last night, and his conversation on the radio had been nothing short of ludicrous. His confused thinking and untimely questions might have been the result of a sleep-hazed mind. Drinking also might have had something to do with it. Neither excused him in my opinion. The little he could have done, he failed to do. And he saw no need the following day to come and survey the scene for himself. I wrote him off as a loss, a casualty of the battle as certain as any of my own wounded.

Intelligence reports in the days that followed indicated that the enemy felt they had lost face. The fight had been their first attempt to take by storm the American position adjacent to Truong Lam. They had fallen back in defeat, not even able to take all their dead with them, which was a basic psychological tactic of the Viet Cong and their North Vietnamese cadre. The only element of the battle they had been able to seize upon was the rather empty claim that the Americans had murdered innocent people in the village. The net assessment from American and Vietnamese intelligence was that the enemy would try again, and try hard.

As the general had promised, reinforcements and replacements began flowing into my small perimeter. The armored cavalry platoon was assigned to stay with me. It was an awesome collection of fire-power, of limited use in patrolling the region but certainly a formidable element in defense. A total of three squads was attached to my platoon, one coming from each of the other companies in the battalion, giving me a total of six infantry squads for maneuver. I also received individual replacements for my casualties, as well as extra replacements to bring my own squads close to full strength. Even the RF platoon was reequipped (they had abandoned many of their weapons in their rush to join us) and reinforced. The RF platoon leader was not replaced, however, and I could not exercise command authority over his men, so

I viewed their presence as little help. Nonetheless, I now had an assembled force of over ninety men, which, in the days of heavy attrition among combat units, approximated the strength of a fielded rifle company.

The three new reinforcing rifle squads were cause for concern. They were not an integrated unit; each squad came from a different company. The men were not the better-quality soldiers I had come to know in Vietnam. I suspected that I was the recipient of unwanted soldiers whose commanders had jumped at the chance to rid themselves of problems.

One man stood out as exceptionally undersirable. He sauntered into the platoon wire showing all the mannerisms of a drug pusher from the South Bronx, his lanky frame swaying to a beat heard only in his disturbed mind. Within minutes he was antagonizing everyone else in the platoon, and I had him report up to me.

"What's your name, soldier?"

"Just call me Prince, man."

"I'll ask you again, soldier—what's your name?— and if I don't hear 'lieutenant' or 'sir' behind it I'll have you dig me a six-foot foxhole."

"Private Edward Pricer"—long pause—"lieutenant!"

"How long have you been here, Pricer?"

"Just got here"—pause—"lieutenant."

"I mean in Vietnam, Pricer, and speed up the lieutenant."

"Five years, L.T." He was getting friendly.

"Why have you been here so long?" I asked, not believing him.

"Because I killed five men in the States, sir, and I can't go home, sir." He was leering at me now.

"Look, private, I'm not impressed that you killed five men in the States. It's over here that your ability to kill means anything. You get back to your squad and keep your mouth shut. If your squad leader tells you to kill something, then you kill it. Until then watch your step. There's not a man here who's got time to put up with any crap from you, and most of us are a lot more killer than you." I dismissed him. He and a few others would bear watching.

The replacements I was getting presented problems of a different kind. They were wide-eyed innocents who had never seen combat, taking the place of men who had fallen in battle in an area that was rumored to be the target of an angered enemy. I had had five years of preparation; sixteen or eighteen weeks had been their transition time from civilian to combat infantryman. I looked to their squad leaders, barely older than the new men themselves, to take care of them.

Hernandez, my platoon sergeant, would be the key there. Unfortunately, a rift had opened up between us as a result of the fight. Hernandez felt I had usurped some of his authority because my orders had dominated the action, not only in the placement of the fire, but in the redistribution of men and ammunition. The latter I had done only when Hernandez was pinned down by fire, but the fact that I had done it at all wounded his sensitivities. Therefore, I had to spend some time repairing the damage. It was my nature to be forceful. It was his nature to be relatively passive until the battle came to him, and then he was a tough fighter. Yet in battle there is nothing more important than unity of command, and I was determined to lead. While I tried to honor the sergeant's responsibilities, I knew I had to lead the tactical fight myself. It was my job.

I saw no need to wait for the enemy to reorganize and pick an opportune moment to strike again. I wanted to use everything I had to confound their plans. During daylight hours I dispatched the armored cavalry platoon, minus the two Sheridan tanks, to sweep throughout my area of operations. The carriers were bulky and noisy, but they could move rapidly if they had to, and that in itself was enough to keep the enemy reeling and off-guard. At night I flooded the area with sweeps, patrols, and ambushes, but I kept the entire cavalry platoon close by the platoon perimeter to react to any concentration of enemy. Additional men called for greater control measures, and I found myself sleeping less and less, trying to insure that no mistakes were made.

The entire region in and around the village of Truong Lam had become extremely active. The intelligence reports were accurate: the enemy were increasing their pressure all around us in an attempt to weaken government control over the village. During this period, my platoon had the dubious distinction of being the most active unit in the 173d Airborne Brigade.

The fog of war is pervasive. As vigilant as I tried to be, I knew it was only a matter of time before a mistake was made. There were six squads to control, as well as the armored cavalry platoon and the still disjointed RF gaggle. Moreover, Vietnamese Regular Army units were infringing on my area. As a platoon leader, I had the problems of the rich: too many resources to coordinate in a limited area of operations. The ingredients for tragedy were brewing.

One moonlit night I received a radio call from a squad lying in ambush: "Tango Romeo Two-Six, this is Tango Romeo Two-One, over."

"This is Romeo Two-Six, over," I answered in a whisper.

The squad, one of my own, had spotted a small element moving several hundred meters from their position. The trespassers were clearly silhouetted through the sniper scope, a device that accentuated whatever natural light was reflected from the moon and the stars.

They were moving along the ridge, outlined against the softly lit sky.

I checked my map for the positions I had established during the night. None of my people was close to the area of the sighting, and all were set in position at that particular moment. A call to company headquarters confirmed that no other company units were anywhere near the sighted ridgeline. Still not satisfied, I radioed the battalion operations center and, within a few minutes, after the operations officer checked with adjacent American and Vietnamese units, was assured that no other friendly elements were within eight hundred meters of any of my positions.

All checks had been made. The squad still had the moving element in sight. The decision was now mine. "Take them under fire with the sniper. Then open up. Shoot to kill." The last statement seemed pointless; we always shot to kill, but it reflected my troubled thoughts over the risk I was taking. The enemy just did not go that way. But no "friendlies" were reported anywhere near us. It had to be enemy.

In the dark, I heard a single shot ring out. Close behind it came other small arms fire, 40-millimeter grenade launchers, and two screeching light antitank rockets. For fifteen seconds a cacophony of impacting rounds tore the ridgeline apart.

And then a frantic voice screamed from my radio: "Cease fire! Cease fire! My God, you're killing us!"

I was horrified as I grabbed the handset and barked my order: "Two-One, Two-One, this is Two-Six! Cease fire, over!" They had heard the original plea, and even as I spoke the melee quieted.

Again the radio spoke: "You sons of bitches. They're dead. They're dead."

"Unknown station, unknown, this is Tango Romeo

Two-Six, identify yourself, over." My voice sounded unsure.

In the next thirty minutes, the painful story unraveled. The voice belonged to an American advisor who had wandered twenty-five hundred meters off course with his Vietnamese platoon. They had reported their night's mission to no one, and although the American had monitored my radio frequency, he never suspected for a moment that it was he we had sighted. By the time we stopped firing, one of his men was dead, and two badly wounded.

I never met the owner of the voice or any of the Vietnamese he advised. I could have been angry at him for getting lost in the dark, something a soldier should not do. I had ordered the execution of those men because the lieutenant advisor had made a mistake. But it happens, and a man should not be condemned to death for it. In war, however, the price for mistakes is dear. And terribly final. Military leaders must weigh the effects of their decisions carefully because usually there is no turning back.

A road wound about four thousand meters from the village of Truong Lam through our area of operations toward the only asphalt road in the area, Highway 1. It was the only supply route to the village, and inasmuch as the existence of the village was an achievement of the Vietnamese government, the burden was on the regime to get supplies to it over that route. Since the village was essentially self-sufficient, there was very little traffic in supplies. But once the enemy made a point of contesting the village, and because there had been a battle that destroyed a part of it, it became imperative for the government to move in some simple building materials to restore the damaged sectors. The traffic meant an additional daily mission for my platoon: a minesweeping operation on the portion of road that was in our sector.

It was a particularly unattractive mission. The men who swept the road always had to be right on it. We couldn't vary our route, which was fixed by the location of the road, and that left us wide open to ambush. One of our basic patrol rules was never to travel the same route twice over any short span of time. However, for the minesweeping mission we had no choice.

And so the game of cat and mouse became more complicated as I tried to find ways to keep the enemy off-guard. We ambushed the sites they might use to ambush us. We swept the area adjacent to the road before the minesweepers came into what might otherwise be a kill zone. But try as we might, we remained extremely vulnerable. Ironically, we were exposing ourselves so that the government could provide building materials for a village populated to a large degree by the families of men who would kill us if we relaxed our vigilance for a moment.

The effect on my men was demoralizing. They knew they were endangering themselves, and they knew instinctively that it was for a vague and questionable political reason. No rational man wants to risk his life for the propaganda benefits of others.

As with normal patrols and ambushes, I rotated myself on the minesweeping mission. Sometimes we found nothing; at other times we found enough explosives to blow any light armored vehicle to bits. On one occasion we completed our sweep to the edge of the adjacent unit's sector only to find on our return sweep that the enemy had come in behind us and planted one antitank and two antipersonnel mines. We couldn't let our guard down for an instant.

The armored cavalry platoon that had come to our rescue on the night of the battle for Truong Lam was increasingly diverted to hauling in supplies to the village. My classmate Larry had begun to fancy himself a fighting leader of cavalry and regretted seeing his men used for such mundane tasks. A few vehicles still went on sweeping missions for me, but they were doing too much damage to surrounding cropland, and I had to stop. There was a limit to the effectiveness of armored personnel carriers and tanks in the Vietnamese coastal plain area.

By the seventh day after the battle I began to lose my reinforcements. The additional squads were returned to their companies, and while I did not mind seeing men like Pricer go, I felt a little naked as my strength dwindled. Even Larry's armored platoon received a warning order that it would be reassigned after one more mission of hauling tin roofing to the village.

I planned on sharing one final meal with Larry when he completed his mission and before he moved on. Over the past few days I had been showing off my mastery of C ration cooking and went to work on my pièce de résistance: Spill off the top fifth of a can of beans and meatballs. Add a can of cheddar cheese, crush in some dried crackers, and lace heavily with Tabasco sauce. Heat slowly over a fire of peanut butter and insect repellent (it burns with a low blue flame) and stir steadily with sharpened bayonet. Canned pound cake and blueberry jam top off the main dish nicely.

The radio interrupted my preparations: "Caravan Caller Five-One, this is Caravan Caller Six-Two, over." It was the first sergeant. I wondered why he was calling. He was not in the tactical radio net and seldom used it for any administrative business.

"This is Caravan Caller Five-One, over," I answered.

"This is Six-Two. Got some bad news for you. Your buddy's been killed. His track hit a mine. Whole crew is dead. Over."

Dazed, I asked, "What wound killed him?" It seemed

important for me to know, as if I had to picture his body in its final state.

"This is Six-Two. Not a mark on him. They just brought him in. His face is blue, though. It must have been the concussion."

"This is Five-One. Roger, over." My radio procedure was meticulously correct.

"I'm sorry. I know he was your friend."

"This is Five-One. Roger, out."

I turned to my meal. The sauce was boiling over the edge of the can, threatening to extinguish the flame underneath. I gingerly removed it from the fire. Quietly I ate my meal.

Larry said he had a girl waiting for him. Well, there would be no more waiting. Larry was gone. His arrival had probably saved my life seven days earlier. It was hard to accept the fact that he had been killed toting tin to Truong Lam.

I took the Kool-Aid I had mixed for him in my canteen cup and doused the burning peanut butter. A bitter smell filled my nostrils.

# CHAPTER 13

# THE LOWLY INFANTRYMAN

It is somewhat unnerving to go about your mission with someone spraying bullets at you. That became typical of the enemy tactic against us during the last half of October. The old stand-by booby traps were still out there waiting for us to take a wrong step, but the enemy was avoiding direct, close-in firefights. They were licking their wounds, but they were not letting up on the pressure.

From distances of five hundred to six hundred meters the enemy would try to catch us as we moved within our perimeter or crossed an open area on patrol. At that range we had little chance of hitting them with direct-fire weapons such as rifles or machine guns, and they were beyond the four-hundred-meter range of our M-79 grenade launchers. The only weapons we could use against such attacks were the company 81-millimeter mortars, of which there were three, all of them located in company headquarters. By the time we received clearance to use them in such a populated area, the enemy was long gone.

It was a frustrating time. Seldom was the enemy effective from such ranges, but a single casualty a day could wipe out a platoon in a month. It was hard for us to see men we knew carried away in pain, with no way of getting back at those who had hurt them. I began to worry about the state of our morale.

But the American soldier has a remarkable capacity

to find relief amid the most depressing predicaments. There was a little of Phil Nail in each of us, and although he was still off recuperating in some hospital, we all followed his example and refused to take ourselves too seriously.

One sunny day found us laboring with the details of our existence atop our barren knoll astride Truong Lam. Our Kit Carson scout, Nhan, was relaxing with a can of peaches, no doubt contemplating a late afternoon liaison with a pleasantly plump widow who had caught his eye while going about her village chores. Platoon Sergeant Hernandez and a small detail were stacking extra ammunition in a little hollow we had dug out of the eastern side of the crest, while a recently returned squad was heating some C rations.

I was busy interviewing a new arrival, Pfc Steve Fricker from Minot, North Dakota. Fricker had the markings of a good soldier—intelligent, alert, athletic— but one of his habits concerned me. He was a vegetarian.

"But the staple of the C ration is meat," I had tried to explain.

Fricker was undaunted. "No problem, sir. I'll see what I can trade for. And one of the guys told me there's a short, fat, delicious banana that grows around here."

As I was contemplating that unique problem, my thoughts were interrupted by a deadly spray of bullets that came zinging across the perimeter. Fricker and I crashed into each other as we dove into my little slit trench. Nhan joined us a split second later, spilling his peaches and syrup all over us as he tried to squirrel into the brown earth.

"Damn it, Nhan!" I muttered. Fricker licked his fingers as another burst chewed up the ground adjacent to our crowded hole.

Nhan was mad. Not only were his cherished peaches wasted in the dirt, but the tempting ideas he had been entertaining about the *mama-san* in the village below were rudely erased from his thoughts. He let go a return fire of eloquent Vietnamese curses.

Since I was unable to maneuver my weapon effectively in our cramped quarters, I satisfied my prerogative of command by directing Nhan to adjust his fire by raising his voice. Encouraged, he let go with an even more searing burst of epithets. In return we received another volley of bullets, but that time they all went high, as if the enemy had been distracted. The Americans, not to be outdone by their Vietnamese ally, joined in with a chorus of American-Vietnamese pidgin expletives. The enemy must have been wounded; their rounds coursed every which way but on target. A tactic had been born. Assaulted by our insulting catcalls, the enemy beat a hasty retreat.

Following up our discovery of the enemy's thin skin, I developed a contingency plan to counter their demoralizing sniping attacks. I briefed the squad leaders. The initial sniping would be countered by a stream of derogatory insults. As they drew the expected angry responses of undisciplined fire, the better marksmen in each of our squads would try to draw a bead on the point of origin. Simultaneously, I would order a squad to close in quietly on the identified enemy location from a well-covered flank. As the assaulting squad flushed the snipers from their concealed positions, our own marksmen would try to pick them off as they fled.

The enemy cooperated, playing into our hands three or four times before they began to realize they were being duped. It gave me no small pleasure to see that our wily foe was, after all, fallible. Piqued at our disrespectful and, in their eyes, unsoldierly tactics in response to their much more professional initiatives, they would stay in place just a little too long, trying to teach us not to be so cavalier. It took a few tragedies and near tragedies for them to learn their lesson. In the meantime, I continued to encourage my men to hurl back defiant insults. It added to their sense of bravado, making them feel every bit as tough as the enemy they faced. In truth, they were.

It also had an effect on the local population. I assumed that one of the motives of the enemy sniping was to demonstrate to the villagers that they could strike at will at the "imperialists." But our catcalling made a mockery of their efforts, and in the end cost them that most important of Asian values, face.

Face was an important aspect of that war. It was a symbol of the legitimacy of the government of Vietnam to show face: the government had to demonstrate that it was in control, that it could nurture civic programs even in a location as vulnerable to the ravages of war as Truong Lam. Accordingly, in the midst of our struggle we received a group of Vietnamese specialists whose job it was to grant face to the government. Called RDs (initials standing for the Revolutionary Development program to which they belonged) by the Americans, their job was to construct facilities and programs in the village of Truong Lam that would demonstrate the stability inherent in the South Vietnamese government.

It was an idea born of American social science, a descendant of our own Vista and Peace Corps programs. The RDs even looked like the people who carried out our own similar programs: young, idealistic, exuberant, full of enterprise and good will. Only their personal side arm, a light carbine, hinted of the possible ill fate of an American concept in the war-torn countryside of Binh Dinh province.

The twelve men and one woman who came to Truong Lam represented to me more than a simple social experiment. Their presence also demanded an extension of my mission. Their carbines would give them little protection from the wrath of the Viet Cong should any of their programs succeed. They would be able to work in the village during the day, but I would have to draw them into the protective cocoon of the platoon perimeter at night. We made a hasty provision to allow them to sleep under a light poncho shelter in the middle of the platoon position, and I allocated one part of the defensive trenchline into which they could roll should we suffer an attack.

The sole woman was married to one of the RD cadre, a rather small man. She worked alongside the team for part of the day, and then spent the remainder of the time preparing the evening meal for her husband and his companions. She did her cooking in the village, although at night I allowed her to join her husband within the platoon perimeter. She was an attractive young woman and was the only female I had allowed within the confines of the perimeter. Her presence was unduly disconcerting to the American soldiers, but as I saw it at the time I had no alternative. The Viet Cong would not hesitate a moment to get at a man through his wife, and to exclude her would have risked her assassination.

Sergeant Hernandez did not like the arrangement at all. He was no champion of the Revolutionary Development program in the first place—"A dumb fucking idea!" was his assessment—and he certainly did not like having a bunch of Vietnamese inside our perimeter. Our Kit Carson scout also protested.

"What's bothering you, Nhan?" I asked.

"No likee," was his curt response. "Nhan smell VC!"

That was enough to keep us alert. While most of the men awake at any given time after dark kept their eyes focused on the outside of the wire, Nhan, Hernandez, and I watched over our guests. The vigilance paid off.

One night at approximately 2300 our little bridegroom stirred from his straw mat and began a slow, deliberate movement toward the ammunition bunker.

Hernandez, lying quietly in the background, allowed him to make his entry and then came to get me.

"Better wake up, lieutenant. The gook's making his move."

"What's up?" I asked.

"The runt's in the ammo bunker." I thought of the three days supply of ammunition we kept stored in the small, hollowed-out pit, enough to blow away the entire eastern portion of the perimeter. The concussion itself would probably daze everyone on the hill, even at the remote ends of our little defensive position. I kicked Nhan awake and we started crawling toward the bunker.

As we neared the opening to the pit, I could hear the man rustling around inside. Peering into the aperture, I saw him wrapping detonation cord around our boxes of explosives. The cord is like a clothesline that detonates instantaneously along its entire length, the charge moving down the line so fast that it is impossible to discern a rate of movement. The explosive force is such that a single strand wrapped around a solid tree will fell it. There was no doubt as to the man's intentions.

Had the Vietnamese been anywhere but the ammunition bunker, I would have shot him on the spot. The risk of an explosion was too great, however, so with a quick nod to Hernandez I dove inside and wrestled him to the ground.

He was now a prisoner of war, and I wanted to ask him a few questions. Nhan, his face full of menace for the uncovered Viet Cong in our midst, interpreted my questions and passed them on: Who was he? Why was he making his move tonight? How many others among the RDs were Viet Cong? What were his instructions? Who did they come from?

The man was no slouch. He gave half-answers to my questions. I was drawn further and further into conversation with him because it was frustrating to use

Nhan as an interpreter. His English was sparse and he had difficulty comprehending the thrust of my questions. There was just enough confusion in his answers to stall the interrogation.

As I moved closer, trying to make him understand me, he attempted to complete his mission. Somehow he had palmed a razor blade which we had not found when we searched him. As I spoke, his right hand snaked toward my throat, the blade aiming at my jugular vein. My reflexes were quick enough to catch his hand as it reached for my neck, and I twisted his hand violently until the razor dropped at his feet.

Enraged, I grabbed him around his throat with both my hands, pressing my thumbs deeper and deeper into the mass of tissue and cartilage at the base of his neck. His eyes bulged and his tongue protruded from between his swelling lips. I pressed harder, trying to force my thumbs and fingers to a meeting through his larynx. I was like a mad animal whose only goal in life is to kill its enemy. My arms shook from the tension in my forearms, and I cursed him in a low, guttural monotone. He flailed weakly at my shoulders, his face contorted in an expression of horror. His legs began to twitch and could no longer hold him off the ground. I hunched over him, trying desperately to squeeze the last of his life from his body.

"Sir, you're killing him. You can't do that." It was Sergeant Hernandez snapping me out of my madness. As I realized what I was doing, I released my hold and let the VC crumble to the ground. He lay there hacking a terrible dry cough, his eyes slowly withdrawing into their sockets. A shiver ran down my spine, and I fought hard to control my voice as I gave the order to tie up our prisoner and to wake the men for the night attack I anticipated. I was once again the military leader, not a kill-crazed animal, although the realization of how close the two can be was chilling.

I was sure a fight was coming. I radioed the one squad that was out, cautioned them to beware of an ambush, and ordered them to move back in. The men within the perimeter moved silently to their trenches. I had the RDs awakened, placed under guard, and moved to the shelter of one of the two underground bunkers within the perimeter. The woman and her alleged husband were also moved and tied up. As the returning squad reached the platoon wire I personally counted them in. We needed no more infiltrators inside the wire.

We were poised and ready when the attack broke at 0100. With the night scope we picked up five men moving through the barbed wire on the eastern side. The Viet Cong sappers were skilled craftsmen who could snake through the most complex barbed wire and mine barriers. I moved over to the flank they were approaching, poised the squad, and fired a flare, exposing their almost naked bodies in the eerie glow of the artificial light. We killed them quickly.

A thirty-second pause followed as the remaining enemy realized their plan had been blown. I used the time to call the company headquarters and confirm that we were about to be hit. Calling earlier probably would have tipped my hand to the enemy, who were very good at monitoring our radio frequencies.

And then the attack began in earnest as a hail of M-79 rounds fell like mortars, dead on our position. I always marveled at the enemy's accuracy with that weapon. I felt sure that given a clear view and enough rounds, they could eventually land one in my canteen cup. They did no damage that time, however, because all my men were well protected in the trenches. Then came the small arms fire; it was also to no avail, although it did give us pause to hear the bullets whirring through our barbed wire and cutting through the steel pickets along the perimeter. The more the enemy fired, however, the more advantage it gave us, because it gradually pinpointed their location.

I yelled an order for the squads to fire only at my command and then tried to adjust our fire in on the enemy's location. They were only about two hundred to two hundred fifty meters out in three separate areas, so it was easy enough to bring effective fire on them.

Artillery illumination rounds were coming overhead at the rate of about one a minute, transforming darkness into day. The brightness crippled the enemy's freedom of movement but left us more exposed on the hilltop as well. In the continuing cross fire, three of my soldiers were wounded, all from the shrapnel of the M-79 rounds. The wounded were lightly hit, however, and in no danger of losing life or limb. The advantage of a prolonged battle still rested with us, and the enemy seemed to sense it; the volume of their fire began to ebb. They made one final attempt to rush us in the interlude of darkness between artillery flares, but we detected the sudden movement and fired off hand-held flares in order to cut them down.

Their plan must have been to rupture our defense with a tremendous blast from the ammunition bunker and then rush us from the eastern flank with the five sappers while we were still dazed; the sappers were armed only with fragmentation grenades, but they had plenty of them. Later we took forty-nine grenades from their bodies. One of the sappers, a young, muscular man who in life would have epitomized the propaganda stereotype of a revolutionary, but who in death appeared like so much wasted clay, was dressed only in a loincloth. Folded within that single article of clothing was a small piece of paper upon which was drawn a rough but accurate sketch of our perimeter defense. Next to the mark-

ing indicating the platoon sergeant's bunker was an X
and the Vietnamese word for "lieutenant." The enemy
could not imagine that the best dwelling on the hilltop
would not be occupied by the senior-ranking man.

The first link in their plan had been destroyed by
the capture of the infiltrator and was further deterio-
rated by the annihilation of the sapper force. But the
Viet Cong were never noted for their flexibility, and
they continued to press forward according to their original plan. However, instead of meeting dazed, dying,
and demoralized defenders, the enemy rushed right into
the protective fires of a ready and able platoon. Because
of a slight twist of fortune over which the Viet Cong
had no influence, the attackers went to their death
rather than to victory that night.

After we had successfully broken the enemy's attack, it was time for us to go on the offensive. The
enemy cannot be beaten if you remain completely on
the defensive; pursuit remains the finishing touch of battle. Even as I began to assemble one squad to flank the
enemy's covering force to the south, I received an order
from company headquarters to counterattack.

The concept of a counterattack is clear enough, but
the execution is quite difficult. The first problem the
leader faces is the act of commitment. By going on the offensive, we had to leave the protection of defensive wire,
minefields, and final protective fires. The opportunity for
surprise was largely lost, particularly at the smaller unit
level. The only surprise option lies in the exact time and
place of the counterattack. Moreover, the counterattacking force not only faces the problem of braving enemy
fire but must move in under the cover of "friendly fire" as
well. Friendly fire can kill just as surely as enemy fire can,
as too many Americans discovered in Vietnam.

So it was not without apprehension that we moved
out to close with our enemies. As we slid out of the

north break in the wire, I noted with a sense of relief that Killigan was on point. I was sure no one had given him the order; he merely took up what he perceived to be his rightful position.

As the squad lined up for the exit through the wire, I looked at their young faces tightened to stifle the fear building up inside their bodies. They were barely men, yet men called upon by their country and abandoned by their more well-to-do peers, about to face a ruthless enemy who meant to put them in an early grave. No words of complaint from any of them. They were American infantrymen and would do the job they were asked to do. No matter that it would not be appreciated. No matter that they would be condemned by their countrymen, or at least those countrymen with the ability and wherewithal to mold public opinion. Tonight they would do their duty. Though they were little more than boys, though they were frightened, though they were not ready to die—they would do their duty. Most of them were labeled as coming from the lower social strata of American society, as if that were something ignoble. I felt proud to be with them and glad to share their company. Their qualities of moral and physical courage, of unselfish dedication to each other amid the difficult jobs they were called upon to do, marked them in my mind as among the noblest of human beings.

We moved out of the wire together, quietly following Killigan as he cut a wide route around to the northwest and back to the south at a point beyond the immediate fires of our own platoon perimeter. We were trying to catch the enemy on their left flank. I ordered the illumination cut off so we could take advantage of the darkness and the heavy vegetation. I was counting on the enemy being confused and largely leaderless, since I surmised that the bulk of the leadership had been cut down in the assault force.

They were still a very dangerous foe, particularly to our small element of eight men. The differing patterns of fire indicated that they had shifted forces; either they were trying to set up to break contact, or they had detected our movement and were trying to outflank us in turn. Night movement is difficult, and we were considerably bunched up; a few-seconds burst from a single machine gun could cut down many of us. My stomach tightened as I considered the possibilities. As always in such situations, my body was soaked with sweat.

As my senses strained to pick up warning of imminent danger, I heard a soft whispering immediately to the front of our column. Killigan had heard it as well, and he brought the file to a quick halt. As each man went prone, I crawled up behind Killigan, trying to get a fix on the location of the voices, which could not be more than twenty-five meters to our front. As I peered into the darkness I could make out a low clump of bushes and what seemed to be a small clearing behind. There could not be more than nine of them, and although that outnumbered my small force, with surprise and a high rate of firepower we could finish the job in a few seconds. I signaled Killigan to stay put and moved to place the rest of the squad on line. I expected the enemy to hear our rustling at any moment and was poised to open fire on a hair trigger.

I was in no mood to take any chances. Already many men had died that night, and I was not about to let the tally rise any higher if I could help it. But before I could follow through on my intentions, Killigan tugged at my arm and motioned for me to stay. Apparently he had read my thoughts and disapproved of the plan.

I glared at him in the darkness. The decisions were mine, and there was no room for taking chances. I hardly felt the need to talk it over. But I could not turn Killigan aside. My fierce look had no effect on him. In one of his rare moments of speech he hissed at me, "Let me check it out first."

I could not deny him. He was not asking anybody else to take a chance. He would go forward on his own. I knew he was no stranger to combat. He was not reluctant to close with and destroy the enemy, yet he was virtually pleading with me to hesitate. Against my own concerns for self-preservation and my bloodlust for the enemy, I gave him a nod. Silently, he crept forward in the darkness.

I marveled at his courage even as I cursed myself for giving in to his request. We lay there painfully exposed to the enemy. The opportunity for confusion and for our annihilation was great. Yet I knew I had to trust Killigan. The minutes dragged by endlessly. My eyes strained to see in the darkness. Sweat dripped from my brow, down my nose, and into the dirt before my face.

Then, as quietly as he had crept away, Killigan reappeared from the darkness. He crawled up to my face and said, "It's okay, let's move on."

"What were the voices?" I asked.

"Family" was his one-word response.

I passed the word to hold fire, and the file began moving. We moved out of position and through the brush to our front. There, huddled in a hole that must have been used as the household garbage dump, were two aged women, an old man, one young woman, and four tiny children. The elderly people had shy, embarrassed smiles on their faces. The children stared in sheer terror. Well they might! I had nearly killed them.

The sight of the family was haunting. How presumptuous, how egotistical of me to assume that the strategic hamlet program was successful, that every night every family made it inside the protective haven of the village. How quick I had been to give orders to fire on unidentified sounds in the night. I, the officer, was

prepared to risk nothing, to order my men to kill innocent people. Killigan, a low-ranking infantryman, was
prepared to risk his own life to be sure that we did not.

I and others like me are trained and commissioned
to lead men into actions that determine life and death.
Our authority, particularly on the field of battle, is virtually unquestioned. We are tasked to lead men like Killigan, to tell them what should be done and what they
must do. We have no obligation to listen to their point
of view. Indeed, to do so might be in itself, or cause to
occur, a failure of leadership. And yet, the American soldier is often much more prepared than his leader to
make a sound determination of what should be done.
Killigan's approach had been wiser than mine. I was too
preoccupied with my own safety and the safety of my
men to consider that there might have been noncombatants in the area. I had succumbed to that most basic
of battlefield strategies: shoot now and ask questions
later. A thousand times I might have been able to ra-
tionalize that course of action after the fact. But had I
gone ahead this time, the people huddled in that hole
would have been dead, nothing but rotting corpses by
the heat of the next day. That they were alive was no
thanks to me. It was to Killigan's credit, and he was just
a "lowly American infantryman."

The details of the rest of that night fade from my
memory, but the operation itself was inconclusive from
that point on. We never successfully closed with the
enemy. They broke into the night, leaving behind only a
few of their dead that could not be safely extracted from
the battlefield.

In the early hours of the morning I evacuated the
wounded. By dawn I reported in the body count, that
most gruesome of procedures. By midmorning the normal inspection visits from higher headquarters were
commencing.

# CHAPTER 14

# THE RAINS COME

Within the space of a month the second major attack on Truong Lam had resulted in a second major defeat for the Viet Cong in our area. Like any organism that has been badly hurt, the enemy had to back away and recuperate before attacking again.

Although our casualties in each battle had been relatively light compared to the Viet Cong losses, they had their effect on my platoon. Combined with the normal attrition from patrolling and booby traps, our numbers had dwindled again to eighteen, and many of the new men were still too green to be reliable under extreme pressure. Among the squad leaders, only Sergeant Donne showed any real strength. Sergeant Robinson continued to have his difficulties, his squad sustained more by the tenacity and example of Specialist Barnes, whose tactical savvy steadied the men. Sergeant James's replacement upon his wounding in early October had been ripped apart by a vicious booby trap, and his replacement, Sergeant Tilles, was a tired-looking veteran transferred in from a unit rotating back to the States. Tilles was old before his time. A wispy mustache, baggy eyes, stooped shoulders, and a pale color gave him a middle-age aura that belied the fact that he was only a few years beyond the legal drinking age in most of the United States. Sergeant Hernandez, still ready to greet the enemy when they came calling, was nevertheless showing signs of strain. We needed a breather.

The decimated ranks of the local Viet Cong gave us a chance to recover. So did the weather. The sunny days had come to an end, replaced by the dismal skies and endless rain of Asian monsoons. Although the rains came in torrents at times, for the most part it was merely a ceaseless drizzle. Although the air temperature did not drop that much, our bodies were acclimatized to the intense heat of Vietnam, and the relative cooling had a dramatic effect on our sense of well-being. Even with the temperature in the low 70s and high 60s, we felt cold, desolate, abandoned.

We continued patrolling. Although the enemy had been momentarily weakened, they were on the move. The rain gave them the opportunity to bring in reinforcements with less chance of detection by our sophisticated intelligence devices. No immediate thrust at the village was anticipated, but the old game of cat and mouse continued.

Nhan had left us for a visit home after the second big fight. Chong joined us, visibly subdued by the Viet Cong attack on his family. He came armed with a loudspeaker set, another government idea to capitalize on the setback to the Viet Cong with a little propagandizing. Each night Chong would set up his equipment inside our perimeter and talk to the townspeople below while playing tapes of nationalistic Vietnamese music. Chong was not the man for the job at the time, however. He was too embittered over his personal loss to use any subtlety in getting his message across. Between Chong's shrillness and the blaring music and the unrelenting bleakness of the weather, I almost longed for any enemy attack to break up the monotony of our life at Truong Lam.

I continued to rotate myself among the patrolling squads, spending more time with Sergeant Tilles and Staff Sergeant Robinson than with Sergeant Donne, who had his squad well in hand. It was Sergeant Robinson who brought us late one rainy morning to a partially hidden dwelling that housed a Vietnamese family of two small children, their mother, two old women, and an old man. They seemed afraid of us, avoiding our questions, and unable to explain a large cache of rice hidden in a small tunnel under their hut. I decided to pick them up for questioning.

It was not the first time I had brought in a suspected Viet Cong family. Normally, I evacuated them by helicopter for processing and questioning at a Vietnamese government center in Tam Quon, the local district headquarters. That was my standing order. But the rains were too heavy for extraction by helicopter, so the alternative was to turn the family over to the two Vietnamese national policemen who had joined us at the beginning of the monsoons.

With much jabbering among themselves, the family walked with us back to the platoon perimeter. The two little boys seemed thrilled to be on patrol with the American soldiers, and even a reproachful glare from their attractive mother failed to stem their enthusiasm. I felt uncomfortable walking with them, particularly when the two old ladies kept giggling every time we stopped to probe for a booby trap. Their presence seemed to make a mockery of our soldierly demeanor.

The national police were waiting for us at the wire. They were young men, slightly built like most of the Vietnamese, with engaging smiles. It was my mission to protect them from the wrath of the Viet Cong, but I had been ordered not to interfere in their work. Accordingly, I turned the family over to them immediately upon walking into the perimeter.

"Thank you, lieutenant," the one named Duc said, beaming at me with a broad smile. He always seemed eager to please, as if it were important that I like him.

I turned away, trying not to look at the family, who

were now very quiet, no doubt realizing that their afternoon had taken a turn for the worse. I hastened to busy myself with other matters.

Try as I might, however, I could not ignore what was going on. Taking them one at a time, the police placed the family in push-up positions, their bare feet raised on large, flat rocks the police had rolled into place for their interrogation. Then, as he scowled at the young woman and spoke heatedly to the old man, Duc slapped the soles of the woman's feet wickedly with a thin bamboo pole. She bit her lip but did not cry out. The children winced in terror at each slap, their thin arms hardly able to hold their chests off the ground, while Duc's partner swore vehemently at the two older women who pleaded for mercy for the young mother.

I gritted my teeth. What did I know of this war, of these people? My orders were not to interfere. They were probably a Viet Cong family. Maybe they were the ones who had cut off the breasts of the old *mama-san* in the village.

Again the bamboo pole sliced through the air and smacked against the red, swollen feet of the woman. The smaller boy fell to the ground, tears welling in his eyes as the policeman thrust him back to the push-up position. My men were beginning to gather to watch the show.

Another blow brought me to my feet. My revulsion at the scene was exceeded only by my revulsion at myself for allowing it to happen. "Stop!" I roared at Duc, who looked up as I approached, utter disbelief on his face.

I snapped the pole from his hand and threw it into the punji stakes ringing our perimeter. "That's enough of that shit! Get your ass out of here!"

Duc and his partner did not know what to do. Sullenly they backed away. "You men get back to your

business!" I yelled at the Americans standing around, ir-
ritated by the scene I was creating as well as by what
had happened.

I motioned for the family to get to their feet. Even
on their faces I could see incredulity, as if they could not
understand why I was interfering. Their eyes seemed to
say that this was their business, a Vietnamese affair. Dis-
dainfully they rose to their feet, their brown eyes glancing derisively at my reddened face.

"Chong," I called to the scout, "get these people
under some cover and give them some food." Bewil-
dered, Chong came over and led the family to a nearby
lean-to while I rummaged through my rucksack for a
dry shirt to drape over the shivering children.

All afternoon I sat and watched the Vietnamese on
the hill with me. Chong, whose own family had been
mangled by the Viet Cong, followed my orders and prepared warm C rations for the family. Duc and his partner sulked under a poncho some distance away, no
doubt planning their official report on the dissident
American lieutenant. The mother nursed her feet, her
scalding eyes accusing me of betrayal and weakness.
The children stole an occasional look at me, but seemed
more intent on watching Duc. The old people's faces
were glazed over with a stoic expression that hid their
inner feelings, a technique mastered long ago in that
cruel country. I watched them all, confused by the terrible war and uncertain of my place in it. I longed to be
pitted against an armed enemy instead of facing this as-
semblage of villains and innocents, victims and perpe-
trators. I did not know who was which, only that I was
mixed in with them all.

Relief came in the form of a warning order received
over the radio at 1500: "Assemble one squad from your
element and be prepared for pick-up by 1545. You accompany."

I had no idea what was in store. I would receive my mission briefing at my destination. I only knew there was an unusual ring to the order. Accordingly, I briefed Sergeant Hernandez not to expect us back for a while, and told him to keep the police away from our prisoners until they could be evacuated. I ordered Sergeant Tilles to get his squad ready.

We boarded the helicopter in a light drizzle. The only thing the pilot could tell me was that he was supposed to drop us at a ranger base camp at the foot of a range of mountains leading out of the coastal plain.

By 1600 I was receiving detailed instructions from a liaison officer from the battalion operations section. Two more squads from other companies in the battalion would arrive momentarily. Adding them to my own squad, we were to form a reconnaissance patrol and proceed up into the mountains where we would attempt to locate a North Vietnamese battalion on the march. I was handed a night vision device to assist me in my mission.

I watched the other men arrive in the light rain. As they alighted from the helicopters, they looked frightened, perplexed. They knew even less of what was in store than I did. From the looks of them, again I suspected that their commanders had selected the most expendable men for the undefined mission. When all were assembled, by 1700, we numbered only seventeen men, two machine guns, personal weapons, and a night vision device. Our mission was to hunt for an enemy battalion that might number up to four hundred men.

Somehow I had to appear reassuring to the men, but I was filled with premonitions. After me, the senior-ranking man was Sergeant Tilles. We were a composite unit, no member of one squad knowing anybody from another. Not only were we unfamiliar with each other, we came from different units where different operating procedures were in effect. We were about to take off for unfamiliar territory, and in less than three hours it would be dark. I had the distinct impression that higher headquarters did not know what it was doing. (That is not an unusual impression held by junior officers. They often suspect that, beyond their own level of command, no one else is aware of what is going on. They are convinced that staff officers give out orders in textbook fashion with no idea of the practical implications. That certainly seemed to be the case that night.)

I designated Tilles the platoon sergeant and turned his squad over to a young specialist with only three weeks in the country. As I gave the operations order, the drizzle halted long enough for the sun to peek through. Perhaps everything would turn out all right. We moved out with some semblance of order, but as we reached a fast-moving stream at the base of our climb I cursed the absurdity of our mission. Since we had no idea where we were going when we were originally alerted, we had not brought along any ropes, which meant we would have to flounder across the swollen stream by linking arms to keep from going under.

The difficulty of making strangers understand the simple procedures that an integral unit performs automatically became painfully clear as we worked our way across the water. The machine gunners set up their guns for security while the ammunition bearers went across the water, leaving the guns with insufficient ammunition. Instead of using silent hand and arm signals as I would have done with my own platoon, I was compelled to shout instructions above the roar of the water. It was a comedy of errors. I found it difficult to account for all the men by the time we crossed because we did not know each other. Three times I counted to make sure we had everybody.

By then nothing was dry. Our maps, hastily issued before we left the ranger camp, were sodden and difficult to read. Our saturated fatigues clung to our bodies and water oozed out of our boots. Worst of all, we had lost precious time making our way across the stream. Already night was falling beneath the clouding skies.

Sometime around 2200 hours, my pace count and compass checks indicated that we had reached our destination. I set a back azimuth reading against some distant peaks, the only objects I could distinguish against the black sky. I could tell by the intersection of the compass readings and the symbols on the map (read by a red-filtered flashlight under my shirt) that we were close to the portion of the trail network we were to watch. A quick check uncovered the exact location, and I proceeded to set up the men.

Whispering my instructions in the dark, I organized the patrol into five groups of three men each. Sergeant Tilles, the ranking enlisted man, stayed with me, our radio being the only link to the support we would need if we ran into the enemy battalion. Tilles and I were located in the center of a star-shaped pattern configured by the five groups, which would enable us to intercept the enemy from any direction they might choose to move. What to do with the battalion once we succeeded in intercepting it was the real problem at hand.

A bare thirty meters separated any two groups of men. This gave us mutual supporting fire, but the few claymores we had with us would be our major line of defense. We couldn't dig in effectively in that terrain because the sound of our efforts might give away our position. No matter which direction the enemy approached from, I would have to shift the position of one of the five groups of men in the dark to bring them all into play. Our unfamiliarity with each other would hinder us badly in such an event. As I gave instructions to the huddled patrol, there was enough light filtering through the partial cloud cover to allow the men to get into position. Before all movement was completed, the clouds had thickened, and we were plunged into total darkness. Even the night vision device was useless.

According to sound tactical doctrine, it was time for me to check the positions to be sure that my instructions had been followed. If we made enemy contact in the dark, everything would have to go according to plan or we would be quickly overrun. But to check the positions was exceedingly dangerous. We sat in total darkness, seventeen of us, looking for an enemy battalion on the march. The men in my own element did not know one another, and they did not know their leader. They were bound to be jumpy.

I had taken the precaution of setting up a running password, a number that would be the sum of the challenge and password. If the number were 10, for instance, the challenge might be 7 and the response would be 3, or 6 and 4, 5 and 5, and so on. I made sure each man memorized the number before I sent the groups out. I also decided to check each position by working my way out from the center of the star-shaped configuration so that I could come back to the middle and make my way back out after checking each group. (To move around the circumference of the perimeter would almost certainly alarm the soldiers and incite them to fire on what they might take to be an approaching enemy.)

I worked my way out to the first position, moving in a low crouch and progressing very slowly. As I approached I was not challenged, so when I came up on the men I admonished them to be alert for an enemy intrusion from any direction. I checked their position as thoroughly as possible in the dark, feeling around for the positioning of their two claymore mines, and checking on the location of their machine gun. Things seemed in order, and after reassuring the men that we would be

all right, I slowly made my way back to my original position at the center.

Even that move was dangerous. Although the center was only a short distance away, the slightest misori-
entation in the dark could bring me past my destination
and eventually put me in an exposed position. Further-
more, the platoon sergeant I had left in the center was
armed and likely to be as jittery as anyone else. Clearly
it was not a night to be moving around, but that was
what had to be done, so I did it. How simple the tactical manuals had made it seem. But I knew that one misstep could get me killed.

My nerves were taut, and my pores were flooded
with sweat. Moving in pitch darkness a man tries to do
the impossible as he strains to see what he cannot. What
an odd sight the face would make if it could be seen in
the dark, the eyes open to their maximum extension,
pupils dilating to catch what little light there might be,
the nose sniffing as if to pick up images through some
type of olfactory radar.

By the time I made it out to the second position, I
heard a distant rumble of thunder. Brief flashes of light-
ning streaked across the sky, offering split seconds of
light, not enough to move freely but enough to orient
myself now and then. The second position was more
alert than the first, and as I approached I heard a whis-
pered challenge. I responded, and was allowed to come
forward. The group was in pretty good shape but only
lightly armed. After checking them I made my way back
to the center of the formation.

Perhaps fifteen minutes had passed since I had
begun my inspections. I began to move out to the third
position. This position, I remembered, had an M-60
machine gun, an M-16 rifle, and an M-79 grenade
launcher. None of the men was from my own platoon.
The fact that they barely knew each other was attested

to by the muffled noises I could hear them making as I approached.

As I closed to within fifteen feet, one of them detected my movement. "Shhh" was his only warning to the others. I came to a complete rest, waiting for someone to issue the challenge. The seconds ticked on, but I heard no sound. I began to sense there was a problem.

The next sound was the bolt and firing pin of a rifle sliding forward in response to a pulled trigger. Both fell forward to an empty chamber. Terrified, I realized that I should be dead, that the rifleman meant to nail me, no questions asked. Only his earlier error in not having chambered a round saved me.

"Don't shoot!" I shouted in horror. "It's the lieutenant!"

But it was too late to stop the momentum of events. I heard a panicky remark from the midst of the group: "Get the bastards!" Then a round was chambered as I flung myself at the sound. Fifteen feet is not far to sprint, but the journey seemed endless. I threw myself parallel to the ground and lunged at the dark figure appearing before my eyes. As I launched through the air, I felt the rounds swish by my outstretched body, nine or ten bullets burning out of the barrel of the automatic weapon. My arms circled the knees of the firer, bringing him down in a heap.

I pushed the hot barrel skyward as the last of the rounds exited the weapon. Although I had pinned the firer, I also had to think about the two other men with him. I yelled out, "Don't shoot, you son of a bitch! It's the platoon leader!"

There was no further firing. Fighting my rage, I tried to focus my thoughts. We were in deep trouble.

The three men in that position had become disoriented in the dark. Instead of facing out, they were looking in toward the center of our star pattern. When I approached them from the middle of the configuration they thought I was coming from outside the perimeter. Fearing an overwhelming enemy force, they had opened fire without bothering to ask questions. Their rounds had gone over my head, three feet off the ground, and continued across the position, grazing over the other platoon groups. Now the others would think the enemy had struck.

"Don't shoot! Don't shoot! Don't shoot! Hold your fire!" I shouted across the perimeter. I could hear nervous chatter from all around. The men didn't know what was going on, and they were scared to death. Seconds passed as I hugged the ground, waiting for the whack of weapons fire winging back and forth over the perimeter as we shot ourselves up in the dark.

Again I called out, trying to inject some authority into my voice: "Hold your fire. It's all right. Everything's okay." Amazingly, no one else fired. I waited, and after a few minutes passed I called to each position, asking if there had been any casualties. Miraculously, no one was hurt.

I turned back to the group who had fired at me. I pivoted them around so they were facing out. I chewed out the rifleman for not having chambered a round before he fired at me, although if he had, I would surely have been dead. I admonished all three men to challenge correctly, speaking to them as if I were giving classroom instructions to a bunch of eager, if not very bright, students. I surprised myself with my calmness.

It was when I moved back to my position that the greatest struggle within me began. Perhaps it was triggered by the decision I had to make. By the book I should have shifted our positions. We were a reconnaissance patrol. We were badly outnumbered by the enemy and had compromised our position with all the shooting and shouting. There were good reasons for moving.

On the other hand, it was a pitch-black night. If the enemy was close enough to get an immediate fix on us, he was close enough to hit us before we could move. Even if he wasn't close, further stumbling around in the darkness might worsen our predicament. Moreover, to effect the move meant I would have to move around to regroup the dispersed men. This was the point that weighed most heavily on my mind. I no longer had the heart for it. I had come within an inch of being killed, shot by one of my own men on the side of an ink-black mountain in the middle of nowhere. I knew the men were ready to shoot anything that moved, and I didn't want to give them a target.

I should have been ashamed of myself. I was too afraid to move, to implement what was probably the best course of action for my men and my mission. I couldn't do it. Naked fear stripped me of all shame or guilt. Fear was all I knew. And I didn't want to move.

A few moments earlier I had been an effective platoon leader doing his job. Now I could actually feel my chest throbbing against the dirt where I lay. I wanted to bury my face in my hands. I wanted to be like the little boy I used to be, hiding from the darkness by putting his head under the covers. I could not think. My body began to tremble, then shiver, then shake uncontrollably. My God, I was going to die! I could not possibly live through the night! If anyone heard my breathing, I was sure he would kill me. Death was everywhere. I sensed it, felt it lying down beside me. I didn't want to die, but death was there, cold and clammy, reaching for me with its icy touch. My pulse pounded in my ears and I felt nauseous. I almost threw up.

The passing minutes, hours, whatever units of time exist in a nightmare, brought no relief. The fear only worsened. I would not live through the night. I was sure of it. Would the dying hurt? I wondered. Would I disappear into nothingness?

When I first went prone, trying to press myself into the ground, I fell close to an ant hill. A few of the ant scouts immediately began a reconnaissance of my body, but it was not until the ant legions were called forward that I noticed them.

As I lay shaking on the ground, thousands of ants began trooping over me, adding to the crawling feeling on my flesh. Still I did not move, for to move, I knew, would put me in the embrace of death. So I lay where I was, heart pounding, skin sweating, ears throbbing, while an army of ants probed and picked at me at will.

Sometime later that night the rains came in a torrential downpour that sent a stream gushing down the mountainside at us. Still I didn't move. My night of terror was not yet over. And when the rains stopped after a few hours, I still lay in the ooze and slime.

First light brought a sense of recovery. Darkness was ending and I was still alive. Only then did the beating of my heart slow. I loosened my belt, reached down into the soggy elastic of my undershorts, and wiped out a streak of drowned ants. The rains had swept them over my body, and where they had become trapped they had drowned. As I removed their dead bodies, thousands of them, I seemed to rid myself of my fixation with death. I had lived through the night, vulnerable as I was. The ants had died, eminently adaptable as they were. Somehow, the irony of it reassured me. One died when it was time to die. Apparently, it was not my time.

As dawn broke, I pulled myself together, gathered up my makeshift patrol, and moved back toward the ranger camp. That night on the mountain, instead of engaging the enemy I had come to grips with my own mortality. That night I had been a terrible platoon leader. But perhaps I would be a better one thereafter because of it.

It was time to bring my patrol off the mountain. We had not found the enemy battalion, and my orders were to move back into the ranger camp. For the better part of the day we moved, the rains pelting us mercilessly, and I wondered how many more ants would drown before the skies cleared.

The morning of the third day I returned to my platoon at Truong Lam. One man had been lost to a booby trap, his leg severed at the thigh. The suspected Viet Cong family was still there because the weather hadn't broken long enough to warrant a helicopter to come in and pick them up. But there was something different about them. A look of hatred had hardened among the adults—even the children had acquired it. But the difference was most noticeable in the young woman. Gone was her look of fierce pride. She appeared sullen, sunken, defeated.

I couldn't be sure what had happened or even if my perceptions were correct. A passing glance between the young mother and the platoon sergeant aroused my suspicion that he had violated her in some fashion during my absence. Whether my suspicions were true or not, I will never know. But I did know then that I would never be able to trust the sergeant again.

Later that day I evacuated the family. I also arranged for the transfer of the platoon sergeant. Hernandez had served the platoon well and had been a stabilizing influence on my own more aggressive tactics. But I no longer trusted him, so it was time for him to go.

I watched the departing helicopter pull up toward the dark and heavy clouds. The very atmosphere seemed foreboding. For a moment I regretted having sent Hernandez away. We were one man less now, and each loss was an appreciable attrition to our small force. But as the skies opened and the rain beat down about my face, I felt glad to be clean of him.

Everything was wet. Fingers whitened, deep-bleached crevices forming in the natural folds of the skin. Tiny streams of water flowed to helmet brims and fell like waterfalls to sodden boots. Letters written home turned to blue pulp before they could be finished. Steam rose from drenched backs and thighs, as body heat attempted vainly to evaporate the torrents of water falling from the heavens. Heat tabs could not meet the challenge of Asian monsoons, forcing us to eat C rations cold, the cascading water from sky, face, and uniform mixing with the thick grease in the cans to form an unappealing sludge soup.

Sergeant Robinson was overcome with discomfort. The big man was not up to the task of platoon sergeant. He was too preoccupied with himself to lead others effectively. Barely able to manage a single squad, he was overwhelmed by the responsibilities of a three-squad platoon. He avoided exposure to the tormenting rains and to the risks of combat that came with the job. Instead he used his rank to excuse himself from the forefront of patrolling or the thick of action. "Sir, I'm in charge of the beans and bullets now, not the fighting," was his plaintive response when I urged him to become more involved.

"Sarge, after me, it's you" was my comeback, but Robinson closed his ears to the warning. I could not tolerate him as the platoon sergeant for long. Again I thought that perhaps I had made a mistake by relieving Hernandez.

A brief break in the clouds brought relief to my problem. Alighting from the resupply helicopter were two replacements: one a young private named Tommy Lee Robson from Flora, Illinois; the other a tough-looking

NCO, Staff Sergeant Robert Palloman from Alberta, Canada. Robson had that wide-eyed look of the newcomer, the look I had worn when I first arrived. He was a kid, the baby fat still evident on his body, and he was scared to death of what lay in wait for him.

Staff Sergeant Palloman was a different story. He did not look as if he feared anything. Almost forty years of age, Palloman had crossed the Canadian border to join an army at war. Before that, he had spent time with the British army in Cyprus, but when that affair ended he tired of peacetime service and terminated his enlistment. By the mid-sixties he recognized the growing involvement of the United States in Vietnam and went south to get back into action.

Slightly under six feet tall, Palloman carried not an ounce of excess weight on his lean frame. Although he had a determined look about him, he was not a gruff man. His pale blue eyes seemed almost kindly, and when he spoke of his wife waiting for him back home, one could visualize a sedate, mild-mannered couple growing into middle age in Smalltown, America. But Palloman had come to fight; that was clear from the first moment.

"Good afternoon, sir. I'm Staff Sergeant Palloman," was his crisp, military greeting.

"Good afternoon, sergeant. Welcome to Truong Lam. What's your date of rank?" The date of rank was good enough; he was senior to Robinson, and by army protocol he became the platoon sergeant.

With Hernandez and Robinson, I had to push to get them patrolling; with Palloman, I had to hold him back. He believed firmly that the only good defense was a good offense, and he was ready to set that example every day. Not only did he take himself out on as many patrols as I would permit, he invariably proceeded to the front of the column, eventually threatening to displace the point man. He exhibited such enthusiasm when he and I went on larger patrols that I had to order him to the back of the column lest I find myself trailing him. He never meant any disrespect; he just wanted to be up front where the action might be. I could have clicked my heels. Palloman was the perfect platoon sergeant.

He came just in time. As October drew to a close, I received orders that I was to be the company pay officer. I would have to leave the field, draw the money at Phu Tai, the Brigade's rear area support base, and patrol out to each platoon to pay the men. The platoon sergeant would be in charge while I was gone.

The rains were heavy again, and I had to walk out of Truong Lam. Air travel was impossible. The day before I was to leave, Sergeant Tilles became a casualty to a booby trap, and I moved Killigan over to his squad to lead it. Although only an E-4, Killigan had all the ability needed to do the job—except that he didn't want to do it. He hated the responsibility. He knew he was a good combat soldier, but he didn't want to be a leader. He let me know in subtle ways: "I don't want that goddamn job."

I closed my ears. Killigan was the best man for the job, and I had a difficult mission for him. His squad would patrol with me to Highway 1 where I would be met by an armored cavalry convoy that would carry me in from the field to LZ English. Killigan would then take the patrol back out to the platoon, at night and in the driving rain.

It was a miserable hike out, and I felt bad about leaving Killigan with a responsibility he truly hated. He cursed me with his eyes as I rumbled away atop an armored personnel carrier in the gloomy dusk. All night I listened on the radio as Killigan led the patrol back. His voice became increasingly foreboding as he made his way through the fierce storm, crossing streams that had become raging torrents since we passed by them earlier.

As midnight came and passed, Killigan's broadcasts became punctuated with curses. He was having difficulty getting his bearings in the howling night. I knew he was hating me every step of the way for what I had done to him. But I had done the right thing. He made it back without losing a man. Reassured, I had my first beer in two months, and then another, and another, until I dropped off into the first real sleep I had had in ages.

With a slight hangover the next morning I started my forty-mile journey down Highway I to Phu Tai. Much to my alarm, I was required to turn in my rifle and grenades before embarking on my journey. In their place I was handed a .45-caliber pistol, a weapon of little use in any arena larger than an elevator. Army regulations had left me naked. Moreover, there was no plan to get me down to Phu Tai. The rains precluded helicopter travel, so with all the dignity I could muster, I stuck out my thumb and hitched a ride.

During the war we lost approximately ten thousand men to other than enemy fire. Vietnam was full of treachery, danger, and outright bad luck, so when the road washed out halfway to my destination, I did not push my luck. After waiting a few hours for a helicopter at a nearby camp, my fellow travelers became impatient and elected to push on in the 2½ ton truck we had been riding in. I chose to stay behind and wait. While trying to negotiate the flooded area, the truck tipped over, drowning three of the passengers and the driver. The next day I caught a helicopter into Phu Tai.

It was when I drew the $17,000 payroll in military script that the extent of my predicament hit me. Here I was in the middle of Vietnam, alone and armed only with a pistol, carrying enough money to tempt any one of hordes of Viet Cong, Vietnamese, and Americans who would kill in a heartbeat for that much money.

Sensing that the sidearm was a dead giveaway to my mission, I discarded the holster and stuffed the pistol under my shirt inside my belt. I strapped the money around my waist. Trying to look like a newcomer to Vietnam, I said nothing about the money to anyone and worked my way back up to LZ English over the next two days.

The risk seemed senseless as I went about paying the soldiers in the various outposts we held in Tam Quon district. But it was the soldiers' right to receive their pay, even if there was no way to spend it. As it was, most of them returned the cash and purchased a money order for me to mail home for them. On the return trip to Phu Tai I broke regulations and carried my M-16.

The paying done, I returned to the platoon. It felt good to be "home" again, and Palloman had things in good shape. A few replacements had come in, and no casualties had gone out. The platoon was pushing up in strength, moving into the high twenties now.

The heavy rains had discouraged the enemy from moving against us. That was some comfort—obviously they were human, after all. Too often they seemed above the constraints of normal men, too hardened to the rigors that wore down the rest of us.

Although it was tempting to rest on our haunches, taking advantage of the respite offered by the weather, I knew that in the long run it would be safer to push more on the offensive. To lie back would only allow the enemy to build their strength, as I was building mine, and to choose the time and place of the next strike. I decided to go after them in their lair.

One of the personnel changes I made was to take Killigan out of his squad leader position. A sergeant had arrived to take over the squad. I passed word to him to keep Killigan off point. Killigan did not like it and was close to the point of rebellion, but I refused to put him back on point. His luck was about to run out. No matter how good he might be, the odds are heavily stacked against the point man. My order, however, meant little. Invariably Killigan would move up to the front, always out there a little in advance of the moving element. It was a role he defined for himself.

# CHAPTER 15

# AMERICAN INGENUITY

In early November we were notified that we would be rotated out of the field for rest and recuperation. In other wars it was routine for soldiers to be rotated off the front line from time to time. Vietnam, however, had no front lines, and units often went for long periods with no respite. That had pretty much been our lot.

The platoon RTO, Pfc Pete Spangler, was the first to spread the news. He had been standing by the radio as the call came in, and in a matter of minutes it passed throughout the platoon.

"Hey, we're going home!"

"Not home, you dummy, but away from this lousy place."

"Where are they taking us?"

"Who gives a shit. Away from here, right?"

And so it went. Everybody was excited, the veterans as well as the new soldiers. I forced myself to think about the defense of Truong Lam during our absence.

A few hours before the helicopter flew in to pick us up, an understrength platoon arrived to hold the position while we were gone. The NCO functioning as the platoon leader seemed quite uncomfortable as I briefed him. He came from a fairly quiet area of operations, and I minced no words explaining the enemy tactics in our section. We would be gone only three days, but to that sergeant it would feel much longer. Judging by the way he spoke, I knew he would function in a purely defensive mode. I couldn't blame him; he had less than fifteen men. I also knew that when we came back the enemy would have stepped up their own aggressiveness, no doubt adding a few more booby traps around the area to welcome us. But that was three days away.

As we waited by the landing zone for the big Chinook helicopter, we were like men about to be let out of prison. A three-day reprieve had been granted. For three days no one would die; no one would get hurt. The men were almost giddy. For as hardened as they were to combat, the prospect of living, even if only for a few more days, was euphoric.

A cheer rose as the big CH-47 helicopter descended from the sky to pick us up. The billowing dirt from the downdraft of the huge rotary blades could not shake the smiles from the faces of the men as they scampered aboard. For three days Truong Lam would not be our worry.

But all was not good news, for there to greet us was the spitting image of Simon Legree in the guise of a pale lieutenant of the finance corps.

"Are you the platoon leader?" he asked.

"Yeah!" I put on my tough-guy act.

"I must ask you to collect all the script your soldiers have. This is military script changeover day, and all monies must be turned in."

I roared above the sound of the engines: "That's bullshit! You can't take their money!"

He was undeterred. "Oh, but I can. Let me read you the lawful order as promulgated by the Commanding General, MACV."

"Spare me, bub. I can read."

Sadly, the paper was official. "When do we get our money back?" I asked, afraid that I already knew the answer.

"In approximately seven to ten days—every bit of it," he replied with enthusiasm, secure in his appreciation of the professional competence of the finance corps.

Military script changeover was an attempt to curtail the black market. Invariably, the script found its way into the local economy. Since the local currency was so subject to inflation, nothing was more negotiable than the U.S. dollar, even if it appeared in the form of "funny money," like the U.S. script used in the war zone. By occasionally changing the script, recalling one issue of script to be replaced by a slightly different script, theoretically the army would frustrate the black marketeers. Only legitimate holders could turn in the outgoing script; others would be left with worthless paper. As it was, the efficient black marketeers usually had enough advance warning to forestall a loss. Only fools like me—who had just run some risk in paying everyone in useless currency—were caught by surprise.

"All right, men," I said, "let me have your attention. Lieutenant Whatshisface here will circulate among you and collect your money. He will have you sign a voucher and give you a receipt. You will get your money back later. Any of you who don't comply—or anyone who threatens the lieutenant—will return immediately to Truong Lam." I sat down amid a spontaneous outbreak of unprintable words. The lieutenant, aware that he was within a hair's breadth of being tossed out of the helicopter, stepped cautiously among the sullen men.

I could understand the anger of the men. There was only one thing they could buy at our destination: women. We were headed for a secluded beach on the South China Sea where an imposing series of steep ridges we called the Tiger Mountains formed an enclave by completely cutting to the shore north and south of the beach site. The enemy's ability to negotiate the terrain was limited. They would be seen long before they completed their journey and would hardly be in a condition to fight when they arrived. Not a thing was there, however, except a low-slung wooden structure without furniture that served as a shelter for the troops. The surf was too rough from the recent monsoon, and hardly a one of us needed to sunbathe. It would have been little more than a sleeping place had not some Vietnamese women proved tougher than the local Viet Cong.

Somehow, they had come to the area, either by boat or by rappelling down the cliffs, and established the only sandbagged whorehouse in that corner of the world. It sat low and squat on a line parallel to the wooden shed barely seventy-five meters from it, separated only by a strand of badly sagging barbed wire that some chaplain must have insisted upon eons ago. It was truly a testimony to the unquenchable will of the human species to make a buck. Tales of the remarkable feats performed by the indomitable ladies were legion. But the hard truth was that they did not perform for love. It was strictly a business transaction. And every one of my soldiers knew that as he turned in his money to Lieutenant Legree.

As we exited the helicopter, sprayed by flying sand, the women waved to us from their unique brothel. Eagerly the men waved back, and then sent off the helicopter and the officious lieutenant with another type of hand gesture.

Perfunctorily, I drilled the men on what actions we would take in the unlikely event the enemy attacked. No one could concentrate, and I had to settle for some ridiculous posturing as we went through our drill. After we stowed our gear in the shelter most of the soldiers shrugged off their pessimism and tried to appeal to the sympathy of the women. The women smiled and giggled at the engaging offers the men were making, but their only answer was a rough Vietnamese translation of "No tickee, no shirtee!" How could the rich Americans have no money?

Dejectedly, my platoon sat on the beach. Could this be our darkest hour after those many weeks of fighting? I regretted having made my obligatory speech about the brothel being off limits.

But there is, in this great struggle of life on earth, an essential justice that shows through just when the wicked seem about to have their way. Like a giant bird bearing a reprieve from the gods, a helicopter appeared around the ridgeline carrying beneath its struggling frame our three-months supply of beer and soda ration. Blessedly, some staff genius had determined years ago that each soldier was entitled to one beer or one soda (maybe both) for each day he spent in combat. Our allotment had failed to come through since my arrival, but in one fell swoop it was about to make good on its promise. Like manna from heaven the beer and soda was descending to relieve the great hunger of the day. What the army taketh away, the army giveth back.

Even before the helicopter could unsling its load and take off, the men were scrambling for their beer. Like so many safari bearers they toted their loads over the wire. The beer could be bartered for favors, and later renegotiated by the women. American ingenuity had come through again.

That night I waited in line to make a shortwave radio call back to the United States in the hope that I could be patched over a phone line to my wife. The wait was long, and I had consumed much of my beer ration well before my turn came. Weather conditions were not right, and I never did get through. It was just as well. I would not have been able to talk coherently anyway. Next morning I woke up in the sand, badly hung over, but thankful for a good night's sleep.

The second day and night passed all too quickly. In

the more relaxed atmosphere of the protected enclave, I was able to talk to the soldiers about their personal concerns. I was getting to know them better, to like them more. Perhaps too much, I cautioned myself. In a few days I would be making hard decisions affecting their welfare. I realized that the more I knew of their hopes, ambitions, and fears, or their families back home, the more it would hurt to risk their safety with necessary orders. But I could not restrain myself. They were likeable men.

By the third day it was time to go. We had been on the beach a little over forty-eight hours, and in a few days the platoon would be riddled with VD. Perhaps that was why the Viet Cong elected to leave us alone: they figured that the women could produce more casualties than the fighting men. However, they overlooked the power of the GI's best friend, penicillin.

The small detachment holding the fort were only too glad to see us. They had been sniped at a few times in our absence but apparently had not ventured outside the wire. That afternoon I dispatched, and joined, the first patrol. Very quickly we were back in the appropriate frame of mind.

# CHAPTER 16

# THE ENEMY BUILDS STRENGTH

The rains ended in mid-November and beautiful weather returned to the countryside. As bright, sunny mornings opened on the lush green vegetation around us, our clothes, our bodies, our very minds seemed to dry out. Once again helicopters could get through on a routine basis, bringing occasional hot food in vacuum-sealed mermite cans, backlogs of mail from the States, and clean uniforms.

They also delivered Phil Nail back to us and with him came a cheerfulness that surpassed even that brought by the bright weather.

"Hello, L.T. How ya doing?" Phil greeted me with a smile that revealed a new cap replacing the tooth that had been shot out.

"Hello, Phil. What brings you back this way?"

"Shit, sir, I had to get out of the hospital before all those nurses found out they were pregnant. Besides, I was getting tired of lying around doing nothing." Nail hadn't changed. He was tired of "getting over" in the rear and thought he should rejoin his friends.

"Look, Phil, I'm sorry I cursed at you the night you got hit," I apologized. "But I needed that radio and couldn't find you."

"Hey—no problem, sir. I know you needed it. That's why I was coming. In fact, that's why I got hit." He smiled and I knew I was forgiven.

I sent Nail off to Robinson's squad. I had another RTO now, Pfc Pete Spangler of Yuma, Arizona. He was still learning the trade and I decided to give him a little more time. Besides, I knew Nail was a first-rate soldier and would be a welcome asset to Robinson's squad. Sp4c. John Barnes, the other mainstay of the squad, would be off on R and R for six days; Nail could fill his shoes.

It was clear that the enemy had taken advantage of the monsoons to build their strength. Signs were everywhere. Patrols were making more sightings and long-range contacts. We were finding numerous tunnels and spider holes, freshly dug in the soft, damp earth. Booby trap findings increased. But despite our vigilant patrolling and ambushing, we could not catch the enemy off-guard.

Through a primitive but effective signal system, which Nhan explained to me, the Viet Cong were able to discover our intentions. If a patrol went out at dusk, a light would go on in a certain hut in the village. If the patrol exited to the north, a certain radio station would be tuned in loudly on a portable transistor. A nearby Cao Dai religious monastery would pick up the signals, light its own lamp, and sound its gong a fixed number of times. When all squads were in, lights would be extinguished. Different combinations of light and sound signals revealed different information about our patterns.

During daylight patrols, children would trail after us a few hundred meters, then dart away to reveal our direction and strength. Later, other children would appear and repeat the process, keeping a steady fix on our progress. Ironically, they were the same children who befriended the American soldiers and often looked up to them as protectors and benefactors.

I was getting worried about our vulnerability. As

the enemy perfected their intelligence system, they would sooner or later catch a sizable portion of the platoon off-guard. As it was, the booby traps, although often uncovered, continued to take their toll.

Because of the limited amount of space within the platoon perimeter, our latrine had been placed immediately outside the wire on the edge of the helicopter landing zone. It was a primitive facility—a bucket under a wooden box with a hole cut in the top—and an unseemly greeting to visiting helicopter pilots, but it was close enough and exposed enough to be relatively secure for daytime use. (Nighttime needs were met by available sandbags.) The exposure necessitated by security also had its immodest side in that villagers exiting and entering the town passed within easy view of our uncovered outhouse. Although it was always my goal to avoid the early morning rush hour as the villagers passed on their way to the fields, I was thwarted by the "trots," which plagued me throughout my time with the platoon. (Bad water, C rations, and malaria pills were a potent mixture.) Occasionally I found myself perched rather ignominiously on our wooden box as several hundred people wandered by. Courageously I returned their smirking waves with my best impression of a MacArthur arm sweep.

One morning Sergeant Donne, the rock-like 3d squad leader, was enjoying the facilities when a peasant woman gathering wood nearby interrupted his concentration. As she suddenly recoiled from her stooping labor with a look of utter dismay on her face, Donne realized something was amiss and jumped from his seat. A quick investigation revealed that the latrine had been wired to a B-40 rocket aimed directly at the seat. Dropping the wooden seat cover to close the aperture would close the circuit and fire the rocket. Apparently, the enemy held nothing sacred.

Staff Sergeant Palloman and I decided to counter what was evidently an increasing freedom of movement for the enemy. We would confound their intelligence system by changing our tactics. Ambush patrols would set up with enough noise to allow the enemy to fix our location and pass the information. Then, after dark, we would stealthily move several hundred meters and reestablish a position. Select patrols were enlarged, and a machine gun added for greater firepower; a small element of the patrol was then dropped off along the way as a stay-behind ambush. They remained in place even after the main element moved back inside the wire. Sometimes we would slip into the rice paddies at night and glide with our faces barely above water to critical junctions along likely avenues of enemy movement. Discovered tunnels were sprinkled with CS, a riot-control chemical, or blown with concussion grenades. Without warning, I would dispatch a fast-moving patrol at first light to swoop down on suspected Viet Cong nighttime shelters before any word could be passed to warn them. We were beginning to catch the enemy.

The enemy retaliated with more booby traps and other irregular attacks. One morning the village chief was caught at the well as he bathed, his ever-present .45-caliber pistol left a few feet away with his pile of clothes. A small nine-year-old boy, no doubt acting on orders from a relative, walked up, smiled, and shot the chief twice with a .22-caliber pistol. Once again, however, the chief survived, returning a few weeks later to resume his post.

Specialist Barnes, back from six days in Australia, stepped on a booby trap and lost his right leg at the hip. Robson, the nervous, baby-faced kid from Illinois who arrived with Palloman, got wedged headfirst in a Viet Cong tunnel as he was clearing it. He panicked, vomited, and drowned in his puke before he could be pulled back out. Another man, recently arrived, sat down beside a trail to take a break and tripped a Chinese claymore with his butt. I hoped his mother would not ask to open his coffin.

The gruesome toll of the booby traps wore on our nerves. No matter how many we found, we knew there were others out there waiting for a misstep. The terror built. It is one thing to rush an enemy in battle and take your chances in the face of his firepower. The experience is frightening, but the momentum of the act compels you forward, sparing you the agony of considering your predicament. Thinking your way through a booby-trapped area is a completely different experience, and much more harrowing.

Moving along, you suddenly notice a freshly smoothed spot of dirt to your front. You look hard, and the three deadly prongs of the antipersonnel mine come into focus, an unholy trinity extending from beneath the surface of the earth to greet your footfall and rip you apart. You look to your right and see a pile of rocks or intertwined twigs—the Viet Cong warning to their own that this is a killing ground. You order everyone to freeze as you strain your eyes to pick out more booby trap clues. Your nerves have turned to steel coils. Your eyes dart over the ground for telltale signs of human tampering: smoothed dirt, an unnaturally placed vine (attached to a pull-pin safety), a thin wire across your path, a broken bush. Time stands still. You're afraid to move; at the same time you want to duck your head and dash to safety. Maybe you can make it before the detonation catches you. But what of the others? You have to get them all out. Keep cool. That's it, bring the others slowly into a straight file. Careful, watch where you step. Now work your way up to the front. Look carefully before each footfall. Watch for nearly invisible wires. One slight tug could bring metal tearing through your flesh like a frenzied power saw.

*Okay, let's move. Stay in line. Don't bunch up. Can't let one booby trap get more than one of us. But which one? Me? Him? Concentrate. Don't think about the explosion. Look! Look! You can see them if you look carefully enough. Take another step. We're almost out of it. Christ, don't ambush us now! We can't move. Concentrate, think of where you would plant them. Look for the telltale signs.*

And so it went. Tremendous pressure followed by tremendous relief as the booby-trapped area was cleared. Then the journey continued, only to bring the patrol to another threatening area. It played on your nerves.

Somehow, the men put on a show of bravado. One day Nhan found a 60-millimeter mortar round wired to a smoke grenade pin. Gingerly he dismantled it and happily passed it to me. "Here, Truong Uy (lieutenant). Number one souvenir."

"Thanks, Nhan," I said sarcastically, and passed the still-live round to Killigan. Predictably, Killigan held it until we came to an abandoned hutch. Then he taped a grenade to the round and nonchalantly dropped it down a well, barely pulling his face away in time to avoid the blast.

As far as possible, we enlisted the aid of the local people to point out booby-trapped routes. At first they feigned incomprehension, but since Nhan was usually along, that excuse didn't work. Sometimes they would pretend not to know where the traps were, but since they were moving through the area, it was obvious that they knew how to get through safely. When they finally indicated a safe path, I would thank them and ask them to lead the way. If they had made a "mistake," they would quickly "discover" it and pick another route.

Perhaps I had gone too far at that point. The thought crossed my mind: Was it a legal thing to do? Was it moral? The villagers were noncombatants, after all. But did they know? Probably. Would they tell me willingly? Probably not, unless they wanted to end up mutilated by the Viet Cong. I couldn't hold their untruths against them. I knew the pressures they were under. But I also knew the risks my men had to take, repeatedly, if we moved through the booby-trapped areas "by the book." As it was, we were losing too many men. There had to be a trade-off.

A leader who arbitrates when the laws of land warfare are overtaken by pragmatic concerns is treading on dangerous ground. The laws exist for practical and humane reasons and I knew that well. But the consequences of my decisions were immediate, and I could not afford the comfort of a philosophical debate on the issues. I tried to behave in a humane manner and did not intimidate, but I persisted until I was reasonably assured that I had the truth, or that my interviewee truly did not know. I owed my men that much.

One day a stay-behind ambush element got into a sudden firefight. In the exchange, one American had been hit in the leg and was bleeding profusely. As I approached the action with the rest of the patrol, intending to flank the enemy, I noticed that the base of the hill we were about to ascend was heavily mined. A frightened farmer crouched in the grass nearby.

"Come here, *papa-san*!" I called. "Nhan, ask him how to get through this stuff." The farmer shook his head in dismay.

A call came on the radio: "Damn it! If we don't get Archibald out of here fast, he's going to bleed to death!"

"Ask him again, Nhan," I ordered.

Again the farmer refused, his eyes widening in fear.

I took out my knife. "Nhan, tell him I'll kill him right now if he doesn't tell us."

I had crossed the line. I wouldn't have killed him, but he didn't know that, and the threat itself was criminal. But I weighed that against the bleeding soldier and the others who might bleed if we didn't get through to them quickly. A leader has no one to look to for advice on such decisions. He must do what he thinks is best, but he must not fool himself as to the consequences of his choice. War is not a series of case studies that can be scrutinized with objectivity. It is a series of stark confrontations that must be faced under the most emotion-wrenching conditions. War is the suffering and death of people you know, set against a background of the suffering and death of people you do not. That reality tends to prejudice the already tough choices between morality and pragmatism.

The farmer led us through. We forced the enemy away and extracted our soldier in time to save his life. We let the farmer go, but not before I thanked him. He looked at me as if I were crazy.

By the second half of November, intelligence was once again reporting the likelihood of a major enemy thrust in our region. As usual, however, the intelligence was not specific enough to pinpoint when and in what form the enemy move might come. To the infantry platoon, where every action is a major action and where every attack or defense is essentially close-in combat, the warning meant little. We were already in heavy contact as far as we could tell. We would continue to be cautious.

Our caution notwithstanding, it was difficult not to offer the enemy an occasional easy target. As we moved on patrol, there was always a point of maximum exposure as we crossed a clearing or a stream or were forced to use a trail due to impassable terrain on either side of it.

Late one afternoon Robinson pushed his squad up an abruptly rising slope. Private Fricker was up on point, carefully feeling his way through the high grass and heavy undergrowth. Robinson trailed him by a few meters, with Phil Nail close behind. Pfc Ron Wilson, an Alabama youngster only seventeen years old, took up the fourth position. Three others followed behind.

Fricker was nervous. For the past few days he had felt his number was coming up. "I don't know what's wrong with me, lieutenant," he had told me shyly. "I don't feel right."

"What do you mean? Are you feeling sick?" I asked.

"No, it's not that. I just feel down, like something bad is going to happen."

"Maybe you've been on point too often. I'll tell staff sergeant Robinson to take you off."

"No, no. Don't do that. I'm the best man for that in my squad. I don't want the other guys thinking I'm yellow."

Fricker wasn't yellow. He was scared. But he was more scared of letting his friends down than of getting hurt. I urged him to take a break, but he had insisted on staying on point. I told Robinson to take him off anyway. Fricker heard of it and pleaded with me to put him back. I yielded.

So on a lovely evening Fricker was cautiously leading the squad up the hill when a machine gun stitched him across the chest. Robinson turned and dashed down the slope, making twenty meters before he stumbled and broke his ankle. Ten meters behind Fricker, Nail and Wilson dove for cover.

Fricker went down on one knee and spun around to face his friends. Blood and air bubbled from the holes in his chest. He dropped his weapon and tried to rise, his arms outstretched as if reaching for help. His eyes opened wide in terror, his mouth agape as blood spilled over his loose lower lip. As the machine gun bullets tore into his back, he tumbled face down, arms still reaching out for help that would come too late.

Wilson took in the scene with horror. "Fricker's dead! My God, Fricker's dead!" His voice rose above the clatter. Afraid that no one understood, Wilson repeated his announcement: "Oh, no, he's dead! He's dead!" He yelled with all his might.

Nail silenced him with a curt "Shut up! He's dead, and that's all there is to it."

Somehow, Nail's words cut through to the hideousness of the moment more graphically than Fricker's death. Wilson was stunned into silence. There was a cursory exchange of rounds, the enemy fled down the reverse slope, and Fricker's corpse and the lame Robinson were evacuated. Nail became the squad leader.

That was all there was to it. Another American had fallen, one of more than fifty-eight thousand to die in Vietnam. The action took a few minutes. There was nothing unique about it. A messy business, to be sure, but one that could be cleaned up by shipping off the body and making a few personnel changes.

But Fricker was dead. A few moments earlier he had been a young man with a lifetime of experiences ahead of him. Now he was just a memory to his family and to us. A few moments earlier he was afraid some of his friends would think of him as a coward. Soon, almost no one would think of him at all. His mother would get a telegram and then a Purple Heart. Maybe I could write him up for a medal, but what should I say? That he was brave because he was afraid to be afraid? That he saved his squad by walking up to the machine gun first? And what did he save them for? So that they might live a few more weeks before following in his footsteps? It was too much to consider. As Nail said: he was dead, and that's all there was to it.

The enemy had known where Robinson's patrol was headed. I had to break their intelligence system. For too long I had honored the sanctity of the Cao Dai temple, a key link in the signaling system since it had the highest tower and the loudest gong in the area.

At dusk that evening, I took a patrol and swept into the courtyard. My men rushed in from all directions, rounding up the disciples working in the temple before they had a chance to flee. We took them inside the temple, a large, open building with a huge eyeball hanging over the altar at the east end of the room. The orb extended from ceiling to floor and half the distance from wall to wall, an eerie conglomeration of papier-mâché and paint suspended behind a tiny, flickering candle.

"Get the machine gun up in the tower," I ordered Sergeant Donne. Nail's squad set up three ambush positions in the area immediately adjacent to the temple. I put the holy men under guard and lay in wait with the rest of Donne's squad at the west end of the room.

All night we waited, the huge eye seeming to glare at our backs for defiling a place of worship. The priests and their staff sat sullenly in the flickering candlelight. No signals went out from the tower that night, and shortly before dawn three Viet Cong came to investigate. We waited until they were within thirty meters. Then the gun in the tower cut them in two. I felt no remorse. We had revenged Fricker's death.

Two days later we moved a little farther out and repeated the process in a Buddhist pagoda. The gentle monks, blind men and women, their white eye sockets and shaved heads symbolizing a sedate resignation to fate, could not deter me from my purpose. The drama of life and death, good and evil, morality and immorality was coming into conflict with the impulse to kill or be killed. I was hardened to my task, yet I knew there were points at which to draw the line. Determining those points was my responsibility, and it weighed heavily on me.

It was not a simple matter of kill or be killed. I had to think of my men. I could not let them be killed because of a rigid morality on my part. But if I compromised with that morality too often, I would become little more than a war criminal, unfit to lead those men. I had to struggle to keep a sense of balance.

Nonetheless, the signaling from the towers stopped.

# CHAPTER 17

# A DAY AT THE BEACH

We began to develop jungle sores. Slight cuts and insect bites refused to heal as sweat and dirt turned broken skin into vicious festering red welts that would not scab over. "Don't scratch," I would say, but could not obey my own orders. Some cases were getting bad enough to require evacuation.

"Make your men use soap," I told the squad leaders, but the water itself was foul. One man, weakened by a prolonged period of inadequate hygiene, succumbed to hepatitis.

"Take your boots off, change your socks, air out your feet," I ordered, but too much sweat and too much walking left us blistered and raw.

The enemy harassed us. They peppered us with mortars, then faded out of range before we could find them and counter. Our mortars were at the company command post, and by the time we got clearance to fire—a caution dictated by the populated region we occupied—the enemy had slipped away. I longed for mortars that I could hold in my own two hands and immediately return fire against the enemy. The 60-millimeter mortar would have done nicely, but it had been deemed an outmoded weapon and discontinued from the army inventory after the Korean War. But the Vietnamese had them. And anything can be gotten for a price.

The price was fifteen cases of C rations. For that we

got a 60-millimeter mortar and eighteen rounds to boot. Not much of an arsenal, to be sure, but enough to surprise the Viet Cong the next time they dropped in. Seeking to preserve our surprise—which may have been an idle dream, since the black market procurement lines probably went back to the Viet Cong in the first place—Palloman and I discreetly placed the mortar under a poncho. Each night, as visibility faded, the two of us would practice putting it into action. We were going to one-up our antagonists.

The RTO, Pete Spangler, tried to take part in our rehearsals, but since there were only a few moments of predarkness when we could work with the mortar unobserved, Palloman and I all but excluded Spangler from our practice sessions. This was our baby.

Spangler had been trying hard to do well. He was a youngster with a swagger, a man-boy who believed that no one else recognized him as full-grown. He counteracted with an air of bravado. On his skinny arms were gaudy tattoos: "Born to Lose" on the left, and a sleek black panther scratching red streaks on the other. Although the radio taxed his narrow shoulders, he would never admit to the strain. He carried the butt of his M-16 on his hip, like a picture book cowboy. But he was just a boy and not a bad one at that.

"Hey, Lieutenant Mac, look at this," he said one day, offering me a photograph album just arrived in the mail.

"What's this?" I asked, not really curious but trying to be polite.

"It's from my wife. Take a look."

I ran my fingers over the album cover, a bright, cheerful yellow. "Looks pretty."

"No, I mean look at the pictures." He was impatient.

"Oh, okay." I opened the front cover. There was his

pretty wife looking at me. She was wearing a stylish miniskirt that revealed full, shapely legs, and a white, frilly blouse that offered a hint of cleavage.

"Very pretty, Pete. I'll bet you wish you were home."

"Turn the pages. Wait'll you see the rest." He was eager and proud.

As I turned the pages Mrs. Spangler appeared in increasingly shorter skirts and lower-cut blouses. Eventually, the blouse disappeared and she posed in only skirt and bra. On the last page her bra disappeared in favor of her heavy, firm breasts. I didn't know what to say.

"Nice, huh, sir?" Spangler was like a boy looking for approval.

"Yes. I mean, she sure looks fine. Congratulations, Pete." I couldn't find the right words. No matter, he beamed. For the moment, Spangler forgot he was supposed to be a tough guy.

That night, the enemy paid us a visit. I was on the eastern end of the perimeter talking to Sergeant Donne, and Palloman was at the opposite end. Between us lay the hidden mortar. Next to it lay Spangler.

Palloman made a quick dash toward the mortar, but a spray of machine gun bullets drove him back into the trench line. The enemy had given away their position by the fire, and we itched to reach the mortar. I tried to make a move, but the incoming rounds were too much on target. Across the hill Palloman caught my eye, giving me a look of utter frustration.

Spangler broke into our frozen stares. "Can I fire it? Can I fire it?"

"Do you know how?" I could have kicked myself for hogging the mortar. In our own boyish eagerness to get proficient with the weapon, Palloman and I had excluded the one man who was now in the right position to fire it.

"Yeah. Yeah. I can do it!" Spangler shouted back

like some high school football player asking to be put into the game.

Jerkily, he ripped off the covering poncho and raised the tube. Across the hill, Palloman and I shouted instructions. Spangler was grinning from ear to ear. The eyes of the platoon were riveted on him.

The tripod properly erected and the azimuth set, the gun was ready for firing. Before we could shout a warning, Spangler grabbed the first round and dropped it down the tube. But he had not removed any of the powder charge, the propellant that determines the range of the round. Up went the round amid the cheers of the platoon, but the cheers soon faded as the round flew out of sight, over the target by a country mile. We strained for signs of the impacting explosion but saw and heard nothing.

Undisturbed, the enemy continued to pester us. "Damn it, Spangler!" I shouted. "Take off three of the powder charges."

"Oh" was his only response. He plopped a new, properly charged round down the barrel.

Again we watched a round sail away, and this time it came down in the vicinity of the enemy. But there was no explosion. Spangler had not removed the packing safety from the nose of the shell.

The enemy was momentarily confused. What were we dropping from the sky on them? Were the Americans employing a catapult? Their fire lifted long enough for me to dash over to the mortar.

"Watch out, Spangler!" I yelled as I picked up a round and tore off the extra charges and the safety. The round rocketed off our hilltop, and this time it came down within nervous distance of the enemy. They lifted their fire and moved off. Our big surprise had fizzled.

Dejectedly, I scowled at Spangler, who felt absolutely terrible about the whole affair. I knew it wasn't his fault. It was mine. I had failed to train him, even though he was eager to learn. I could chalk it up to experience, but nevertheless I was concerned. The enemy would find those rounds and give them back to us in the most unpleasant way they could devise. Spangler avoided me the rest of the night. I was still too angry to kid him out of his guilt feelings.

By morning my mood cleared. A beautiful, bright day was forming and the sun was burning into my fatigues. Palloman and I inspected the platoon. The jungle sores were looking worse. From the extended period of rain, the softened skin had puckered, prune-like. Following that, the intense postmonsoon heat made the men vulnerable to skin tears from the undergrowth, equipment webbing, and insect bites, which refused to heal in the endless sweat. Two of the men looked very bad.

I thought of the ocean only a short distance from our position, barely out of sight beyond the ridge rising to the east of the village. Occasionally a patrol would take us in sight of its beautiful beaches: white, unspoiled sand against an azure blue sea. It was a stunning sight, a wonderful area for a resort had it been anywhere but in Vietnam.

The more I considered the ocean, the more I was inclined to send a few men in that direction. The saltwater would be good for the sores, or so my sparse medical knowledge told me. A quick consultation with Sp4c. Skipper Shives, the new medic from Portland, Oregon, confirmed my guess. (He was probably guessing too, but in such ways great decisions are made.) Besides, I felt that a quick dip in the ocean would do wonders for the morale of the men. If the first trip to the ocean worked out well, I could eventually rotate the entire platoon through the experience, with perhaps some overall benefit. The idea hardened into a plan.

The two jungle sore cases were receptive to the idea.

I only had to find four others to go so I could send off a reasonably sized patrol that could defend itself. Sergeant James, the leader of 1st Squad, returned from the hospital after being wounded in early October, was a qualified lifeguard; he volunteered to lead the element. Surprisingly, King, the soldier who had threatened my life with an M-79 round, asked to be included. Two more, and there would be enough to send out a patrol.

Only volunteers were asked to go on that patrol, but the rest of the men were not inclined to volunteer. A patrol to the beach was still a patrol, with all the attendant risks of booby traps, ambushes, and other enemy contact. But I would not send out only four. I began to gin up support.

"Why don't you go, Spangler?" I asked.

"Don't want to, sir." Spangler was still dejected.

"Aw, go on. You could use a break. Besides, they need a good radioman with them." I was trying to flatter him.

"I don't need a swim. I just need some Zs."

"You may not need a swim, but you sure could use a bath." I was smiling at him.

"Well, okay. I'll do it for the rest of them." That made five.

The sixth was a little tougher. I wanted another strong swimmer present, so I focused on Sp4c. Mark Evans of Joplin, Missouri. Evans's close friend, Ron Wilson, had fingered him as a high school swimmer. Wilson and Evans were inseparable. Both were under twenty and came from tight-knit rural families. They had hit it off right from the start.

"I hear you're a swimmer, Evans," I probed.

"Yes, sir, I am," he responded politely.

"Want to go on the beach patrol?"

"No, sir. Truth is, I don't like the beach. Did all my swimming in a pool."

"Oh!" I was stopped.

I tried again. "Well, I can't send that patrol unless there're a few strong swimmers along. That water could be rough."

Reluctantly, and only gradually, Evans agreed. I had never had to sell a patrol before. I had always just given the order. But this mission was, in my mind at least, a benefit. I was proud of my salesmanship.

I knew there were risks out there, primarily from the enemy, but also from the water. I cautioned James, the squad leader, to clear the area before they set up, and then told him to leave four men guarding any two men in the water. As an afterthought, I added: "And be careful of the water. That sea looks calm enough now but don't trust it. Knee-deep and no more."

My instructions complete, the patrol moved out. By 1400 they arrived at the beach and I received the call from James at the platoon base.

"Bravo Three-Six, this is Bravo Three-One. We've checked the area, and all is clear, over."

"This is Bravo Three-Six, roger. Make sure you establish two strong defensive positions, over."

"Wilco, over."

"And make sure you check that water, over."

"Wilco, over."

"Three-Six out." I terminated the transmission.

Ten minutes later the radio sputtered an inarticulate message from James. He was incoherent and it was thirty seconds before I could even recognize his voice. He was calling for help. His voice was a high-pitched shrill and he was choking on sobs. Something terribly wrong was happening.

Finally his message came through: he had been caught in the tide and was barely able to fight his way back to the beach. He couldn't collect his thoughts well enough to tell me what had happened to the others. I knew I couldn't wait any longer and immediately yelled to a squad to prepare to move out. Within sixty seconds we were out of the wire, proceeding directly toward the beach almost in a dead run. Had the enemy been waiting anywhere in ambush, we surely would have been annihilated. But at that moment I only wanted to get to the beach. While we were moving, I put out a radio call to the company commander to send a helicopter to the beach position as rapidly as possible.

The journey was a nightmare for me. I ran my men as hard as they could go. They were gasping for air, but I wouldn't let them rest. I felt as if I were moving in a dream where my feet had turned to anvils and I couldn't get up any speed. As we ran, I cursed myself for having sent my men to the beach.

The scene that greeted us was ugly. James was still sobbing on the sand. A few feet away lay a second soldier, completely exhausted, wretch and vomit emitting from his mouth in a foul stream. The two security men sat frozen at their weapons, shocked by what they had seen, but too wary of the enemy to move from their guns in the absence of orders from the squad leader. Two men were missing, Spangler and Evans, the two men who had reluctantly agreed to go on that patrol.

My eyes strained for a view of my men somewhere in the surf. They weren't there. Choking back his sobs, James told me that two men had been sucked out to sea, screaming for help. I fought an impulse to jump into the sea, then lost control and bounded into the surf only to be pulled back by one of the soldiers from my own patrol. At that moment the helicopter I had called for came in. Ironically, its load was two Red Cross women (known in local parlance as "Donut Dollies") who had been on their way to bring a little cheer to the men in one of the outposts. They disembarked while I scrambled aboard to see if I could spot my men from the air and pull them from the sea. It was a futile hope. Although we flew repeatedly over the area adjacent to the shore, I couldn't catch a glimpse of either man. As the fuel supply burned low I reluctantly ordered the helicopter back to shore.

Alighting from the aircraft, I saw Spangler lying face-up on the beach. His eyes were half open; a blank expression covered his face. He saw nothing. He was dead.

Helplessly, I stood over his body. The drowned have a terrible look to them. The surf lapped at his feet, flapping his ridiculous fatigue pants around his ankles. His arms lay useless at his sides. His lips were pale blue, ghastly against his ashen face. Slowly, foam bubbled up in his mouth, seawater escaping from flooded lungs.

*Get up, Spangler! Get up! You're not dead!* The words raged in my mind, but did not pass my lips.

My eyes rose to the two American women sitting on the beach, averting their eyes from Spangler's body. Inexplicably, my anger turned toward them. What were they doing there, anyway? What did they expect to see in Vietnam if not death? They and their silly games they organized to entertain the men. Didn't they know these men had no time for games?

Rage was beating in my chest, but it was rage at my own stupidity. I was conscious of the men looking at me and of Spangler's bubbling corpse lying at my feet. For a moment my eyes watered, but I caught it. I turned to James. "What happened?"

Four men had entered the water. The undertow had caught them immediately and within seconds they were well over a hundred meters out to sea. James, a strong swimmer, had been able to swim back to shore. Evans put up a valiant struggle, but got tired and was swept out to sea, screaming for help as he realized he couldn't make it. The other soldier miraculously made it to a floating palm tree and paddled it over to Spangler.

Together they tried to work the tree in to shore. The going was tough, but finally they made it. As Spangler tried to lurch out of the surf, his energy gave out and he lay back down in the water. Again he was swept out to sea. The random beating of the surf eventually brought him back, but too late.

I could not criticize James. He had not followed my instructions, but the fault was mine, not his. I had built the idea into a plan, and then ordered its execution. In so doing, I had executed Spangler and Evans. Wearily, I trudged back to Truong Lam. I felt a hundred years old. No tragedy in that godforsaken country had hit me so hard. It was my fault. I was the cause of two deaths: in the name of good intentions, I had talked those men into dying. I staggered under the thought. The cost of leadership had finally been too high and I couldn't bear it. I didn't consider myself fit to lead. But the job was mine and I couldn't quit. For better or worse, I had to do it.

That afternoon we inventoried the dead men's gear. Evans was missing $500, back pay he had been hoarding to send home. Wilson believed Evans had kept it rolled in a rubber band in his pocket. Two days later, when we found Evans's bloated body several kilometers up the beach, pants and money were gone.

As I went through Spangler's gear, I came across the pictures of his wife he had shown me so proudly. I tore them up and threw them in the dirt. His belongings were going back to his mother, whom he had identified as his next of kin. He had been married too briefly to think of his wife in that way. He was just a boy—with two manly tattoos.

# CHAPTER 18

# THANKSGIVING

Wilson was crying. The loss of Evans, his close friend, had affected him deeply. Ashamed of his tears, he hunkered down behind his machine gun at the strong-point on the south side of the perimeter.

Night had fallen and I had yet to designate a replacement for Spangler, which left me without an RTO. Perhaps I could not yet accept his death. Carrying the radio, I went out to be with Wilson. He avoided my eyes, trying not to show his tears, so the two of us looked off into the moonlit darkness. We talked of several things, mostly me talking and him listening, before we honed in on Evans's death.

Although Wilson did not appear to be an overly religious man, I sensed that the only way to console him was to explain the death as God's will. Personally I could see no point in that proposition. Evans's death had served no purpose; as far as I could tell, it had been a blunder that began with my determination to send a group of my men to the beach. But the guilt I felt was bearing down on me, and perhaps I was trying to make peace with it by bringing Wilson through his grief.

I spoke of Evans's goodness and tried to draw from that a benevolent interpretation of his death. Evans was at peace now, I told Wilson; he was no longer part of a nightmarish war. Although I couldn't follow the logic of my own words, they seemed to lighten Wilson's load.

He began to talk; together we groped for meaning in a man's death. I did my best to conceal my own skepticism and agreed with everything he said. Somehow we came to the conclusion that Evans's death was a good thing: it must be good if God willed it.

By then I wasn't sure who was consoling whom. Sometimes words aren't important for their content, but only for their being said, and whatever we said that night seemed to be good for both of us. Although I couldn't excuse myself for the drownings, I realized that I owed it not only to Wilson, but to the whole platoon, to put the incident behind me.

The enemy chose that moment to punctuate my new resolve. As Wilson and I were talking, I was disassembling the radio so I could clean the internal parts that got wet at the beach. Suddenly small arms fire from a close distance outside the wire chewed into the sandbags to our front. I dived for cover, spewing several tiny pieces of radio into the dirt. As Wilson opened fire with his gun, I groped frantically, trying to find the pieces and reassemble the radio.

Miraculously I managed to find the parts, wipe them off, and stick them back in. Equally miraculously, Wilson took a round in his helmet that followed the crease between the steel pot and the plastic helmet liner and exited the rear without hurting him. Perhaps there was something to this religious talk after all. At any rate, the brief attack had a healing effect on both Wilson and me. As the enemy faded away, we both realized that our immediate concern was with the living. We could mourn the dead, but we could not dwell on them; we had to look after ourselves.

The next morning I appointed Killigan the RTO. He had continually disobeyed my order to stay off point; he would diligently take up this post whenever his squad moved out. The way he defined it, that was his job. As my RTO he would have to stay with me, and there was no way I would allow the radio to be exposed on the point. Moreover, Killigan was one of the few soldiers remaining since my arrival in August. I knew that the odds were heavily stacked against the point man, and Killigan had taken more than his share of risks. I would put him with me.

Killigan was furious. He scowled, hissed, hardened his eyes, and looked surly. "Okay, Killigan, I heard you out," I said. "Now get the goddamned radio and stay next to me until I tell you different."

He was unhappy, but he was a good soldier. He would follow my orders. With a look that could stop a bull in his tracks, he picked up the radio and threw it on his back. I had a new RTO.

The enemy was getting bold again. Toward the end of November, the ARVN base camp in the region to our south was hit and overrun. We lost radio contact with the defenders, and in the morning after the fight we were ordered to push in a relief force.

With some apprehension, we approached the camp from the northeast. The position appeared much like my own, slightly bigger, but juxtaposed to a village below the hill on which it was situated. A great wailing rose from the hilltop as women from the village mourned their dead husbands. The smell of death was overwhelming. The enemy had fled, leaving behind thirty ARVN dead. Not a single allied soldier was alive.

As we neared the camp's perimeter, we came upon the only remaining Viet Cong, a boy of about eighteen. He was dead. He hung suspended by a rope attached to the perimeter wire, feet on the ground, body drooped but held upright by the tension in the rope which ran from the wire, circled his torso three times, and then trailed off to the ground. His mission had been to pull back the barbed wire with the rope, using his body as a counterweight. His body swayed delicately back and forth in the gentle breeze. An army of ants formed a column up the strand of rope to his eye sockets, and already were eating his eyeballs. Grotesquely, he gaped up at the sky, still at his post, committed even in death to his mission of pulling down the wire so his unit could pass over.

Only the screeching widows were alive on the hill. The ARVN had stopped patrolling, the wives told Nhan, hoping to preserve their strength. Unchecked, the enemy had massed and closed for the kill. Only the boy at the wire had been lost. The ARVN had been slaughtered.

I called in my report to battalion headquarters. My mission was to hold until a Vietnamese force came to our relief. As we gathered up the dead, the village below us began to break up as its occupants moved out of the now unprotected area. The enemy had won there; the village could not be held.

Losing patience with the wailing women, I told Nhan to quiet them down. Their high-pitched screaming was straining my already taut nerves. When one woman persisted, I turned to her and barked, "For Chrissake, *mama-san*, shut up!" She quieted. I should have felt remorse at interfering with her grief, but I welcomed the silence. As we left the hill later that day I vowed to continue patrols in my own sector. There was no future in giving up the initiative.

On Thanksgiving Day the army flew us in a hot meal with all the trimmings. Turkey and stuffing arrived in sealed mermite cans, along with cans of mixed nuts and even a container of mashed-up mince pie. Only the fresh milk didn't fare well, souring in the hot climate before it reached us.

I gathered in the platoon for a few moments to give

them a Thanksgiving message, taking a chance on offering a massed target to the enemy. As I looked around, I realized how few faces were left from my early days. Many of them looked so wide-eyed and young. I was now the hardened veteran.

"I would like to give thanks today for all of us being here. We are grateful for each other's presence and support. We are thankful for a respite in our struggles so that we can enjoy a good meal together, as friends. We are, above all, thankful that our families are safe and together, and able to enjoy a Thanksgiving meal in the United States, away from all this and secure in the knowledge that we will do our utmost to keep them safe. Amen. All right, spread out and get your chow by squads, one at a time."

It was the closest I came to a prayer or a justification of our being there the whole time I was in Vietnam. Somehow I sensed that the men appreciated it.

# CHAPTER 19

# "JUST LIKE YOU AND ME"

Company headquarters called one day in early December to give the platoon a mission. We were to conduct a dawn raid on a suspected platoon-size enemy stronghold to the north outside our area of operation. The company would establish a blocking position north of the enemy while we punched in from the south. The mission would require a night march of some distance in unfamiliar terrain.

Leaving only a residual force under Palloman's control, I took the bulk of the platoon and set off at three hours after sunset. The night was particularly dark, the moon having set early, and the going was sporadic and slow. We were to reach an assembly area to the immediate south of our objective just before first light. We would take cover and rush in at dawn.

Rather than take a direct route and inadvertently tip our hand early, I elected to swing wide to the west before cutting back on a northeasterly track. We went through several rice paddies and across several streams before getting back into heavy undergrowth for the final leg of the journey.

I had studied the map all afternoon, for at night it would be of little use. Although I could always stick my head under a poncho and use a red-filtered flashlight, it would be almost impossible in the darkness to orient our location by the adjacent terrain. Instead I would rely on memory, pace count, and a luminous compass for navigation. I knew that I took approximately one hundred thirty-five steps for every one hundred meters I moved. By dropping a stone in my pocket after each hundred meters, I could keep a rough count of distance traveled. I also knew from the map that by proceeding on fixed azimuths, I would cross a certain number of trails, streams, and rice paddies. They would confirm my pace count.

But it is easy to become confused in the dark. Movement takes place over hours, not minutes. Unsuspected obstacles crop up in the direction of movement, and detours have to be taken. The leader moves up and down the column a number of times, retracing his steps and complicating the pace count.

About one o'clock in the morning we struggled out of an irrigation canal. According to my count, it was time to turn northeast. Quietly, I turned the point man and brought the column around. Killigan tugged at my arm.

"You're turning too soon." He was sure.

I stopped and considered what I was doing. Killigan had a sixth sense for that kind of thing, whereas I was a city boy. My field movement experience was learned, but Killigan was born with it. I could not take his advice lightly.

I strained to recall our movements during the past few hours, all the starts and stops, the detours, the prominent terrain features. All seemed to check out. "No, I think we're all right."

Killigan brought his face close to mine. "No, I'm telling you, this is a freshly dug irrigation ditch. We've got a couple of hundred meters to go."

If we were as far off as Killigan thought, we were moving into dangerous territory. Turning on the azimuth prematurely could bring us to the enemy before we knew it or, worse still, into other American units primed and ready to kill whatever walked in on them.

Looking at the distant mountain range beyond the coastal plain, I could make out faint outlines of peaks. I could fix an azimuth on two of them, then reverse the azimuth and trace two lines, one from each peak, back to my own location.

By duplicating the measurement on the map, I could place myself at the intersection of the two lines on the map.

The theory was sound, but there were a couple of impediments. First of all, I had only shadowy glimpses of the mountaintops. I could identify them by contour lines on the map, lying with my head under a poncho, the red-filtered light from my flashlight barely illuminating the wrinkled map in front of my nose. Then I would have to allow for the magnetic deflection between the map's grid north and the pull on the needle from magnetic north, thereby compensating for the deflection. Complex in theory, the procedure was even more complex in application. Nonetheless, I persevered and, to my great comfort, decided I was reasonably accurate in our movement.

"Shit, I still say we're turning too soon" was Killigan's comment on my navigational efforts.

The decision was mine to make. I was torn between Killigan's certainty that I was off and the confirmation of my double check. Instinct told me to trust Killigan; logic told me to trust myself.

"That's enough, Killigan. Let's move out." I had made my decision.

"You're going to get us all killed" was his parting comment.

The words hit me hard. They filled me with fear, self-doubt, and disappointment that the man I rated as the best soldier in the platoon had such little faith in my leadership. Nevertheless, I was obstinate. I pushed the platoon on in the darkness, determined to prove my point, yet aware that if I was wrong, then Killigan was dead right.

I bit my lip and concentrated on counting the pace. The stones piled up in my pocket, and each obstacle in our path was like a curse. I kept staring into the darkness, trying to make out shapes that I might recall from my map study, but my imagination played tricks on me. Trees loomed larger than life. Rice paddies appeared, and I imagined lakes. Trails memorized earlier piled up like a network of worms in my mind. I was trying too hard.

Finally I stopped looking, relying only on the pace count and the azimuth. We were moving blind now, each man barely able to see the dim outline of the person walking to his front. The point man relied on whispers from me: "Move left, a little right . . . straight ahead."

Killigan's silence was ominous. I wondered what he was thinking. Did he want me to be wrong, to prove that he was right? Could he be that pigheaded? Yes, I decided, he could—and would go to his death with a smug look on his face.

At 5 A.M. my pace count was reached. I moved the men on line behind a clump of bushes and waited for the dawn. Slightly encouraged by the fact that we had not been fired on during our movement, I waited to see how far off we might be.

As the first light broke, I stopped blinking. The world began to unfurl from its blackened cloak. I could gradually make out shapes, then objects, then terrain features: a rice paddy to our right, a grassy clearing to our front, heavy forest beyond. My map lay on the ground before me.

My heart began to beat rapidly, and I was filled with elation. We were less than twenty-five meters off our destination! Yes, I was sure of it. There was the slight slope beyond the forest. We had made it in! Our target lay to our front. The men lay prone but were poised for the attack. While I looked to the dawn for reassurance, they feared what it might hold for them. Their faces were taut.

Avoiding a look at Killigan lest I gloat too much, I moved to the radio and called in our intent to move. At a wave of my arm, the platoon rose in the morning mist, and a line of grim-looking men swept in on the enemy.

We closed in fast, making twenty-five meters before the first movement was made by the enemy. On line, just as described in the tactical manuals on final assault, we opened up. Several of the enemy flopped to the ground. A sporadic return fire opened up as we rushed the final twenty-five meters. The fire was ineffectual; the enemy was dispirited. We had caught them by surprise, and they were shooting high. I saw a few more of them fall as we drove the attack home. None of my men was hit. The enemy broke and ran, moving away from us as rapidly as they could—right toward the rest of the company lying in wait three hundred meters beyond.

I led the sweep over the position. Pursuit, or at least the appearance of it, would put the enemy in full panic. We chased them for seventy-five meters; the momentum of their flight would carry them the rest of the way. It had been easy.

Elated, I moved back to consolidate our position. An unharmed Viet Cong was in tow by two of my men. His weapon had been smashed by a round; unable to fight or flee, he had thrown up his hands. Quickly I motioned for Nhan to come over.

"Ask him if he's got any buddies on flank security," I instructed Nhan.

A rush of Vietnamese words ensued, only to be answered by "*No bic!*," an American-Vietnamese slang version of "I don't understand."

"Goddamn it! He's speaking Vietnamese to you. Answer him!" I shouted in the prisoner's face.

Nhan asked him again. The man turned his face away defiantly.

My anger was rising. After my worries of the night before about finding our way to the target, and the successful attack that followed—everything could be overturned by the arrogant obstinacy of one prisoner. Killigan, seeing the way my face was flushed, made the quiet comment: "Don't be mad, lieutenant. He's just a soldier, same as you and me."

Damn him, he was right! I would hope to do the same if I were in the shoes of the captive. Killigan, the quiet man who disavowed all pretense at leadership, once again had made me aware of the fragile superiority of my own leadership. I stopped my questioning, ordered the prisoner tied up, and turned my attention to the consolidation of our position. Small arms fire in the distance signaled the successful conclusion of our operation.

There were two wounded Vietnamese, one of them a woman who glowered defiantly at us as we bandaged her arm. Four Viet Cong lay dead. Looking at enemy dead is an eerie sensation. I had done it often, yet the emotions it evoked in me were disturbing. Could it be—repugnant thought that it was—pleasure that one feels at the sight of an opponent's body? How could a civilized man feel such a thing?

Perhaps the emotion was born of relief. Ground combat is personal, not like dropping bombs from thirty thousand feet on impersonal targets. It is a primordial struggle, you and the other guy exchanging rounds at a few-meters distance. Emotions flow with an intensity unimaginable to the nonparticipant: fear, hate, passion, desperation. And then—triumph! The enemy falls, lies there lifeless, his gaping corpse a mockery to the valiant fight he made. Your own emotions withdraw, replaced by a flow of relief and exhilaration, because he is dead and not you. You pass over the lifeless form to repeat the intense struggle with the next enemy, the flood of emotions hitting you again with a rush that rises above the sounds of battle.

Do that once, twice, three times, and repeat it again later in the day. Do the routine the next day, then again. Soon the emotions become confused. The sense of relief is identified as pleasure in being alive, and life itself is purchased at the cost of someone else's death. Kill or be killed: the emotional result is pleasure at the sight of the enemy dead. Yes, that must be the reason for the sensation—a celebration of life, like getting hungry at a funeral. Or perhaps it is a sign of being at war too long: the essence of humanity replaced by survival of the fittest.

Had I been at war too long? Had I ever not been at war? The thoughts were disconcerting, but there was no time to ponder them now. It was time to focus on the details of the present, the quest for survival. Redistribute the ammunition. Search the enemy dead for papers. Round up the captured weapons. Form a perimeter defense, 360°. Call in a status report. Check out the men. Eat breakfast, one out of every three men eating at a time. That—not philosophical questions as to what we were doing and why we were doing it—was the stuff of life.

Something was wrong with the enemy bodies. Two had been killed cleanly in the brief firefight by wicked wounds that quickly destroyed vital organs. But two bore mysterious wounds—a neat hole in the middle of the forehead, a square of skin hanging open like a trapdoor in the front, a gaping hole like an exploded watermelon in the back; lesser wounds, disabling but not killing, appeared elsewhere on the bodies. Something was wrong. I looked closer: powder burns on the forehead indicated the killing weapon had been fired at point-blank range. The caliber was large, not an M-16 rifle. It was a .45-caliber pistol that had done it. Only one man carried a .45 on that operation: the medic. It was a medic's traditional weapon, ostensibly for self-defense.

Shives, the only "noncombatant" in the platoon, was my suspect. He was the one who patched up the gore. He was the one who sat with his dying buddies, trying to stem the flow of blood or reattach a leg. He heard their last words, tried to stifle their screams. Perhaps it had been too much for him. I called him over to talk.

"How many enemy wounded are there, Doc?"

"Two, sir!" Shives answered.

"What about the dead, Shives? Was there any chance of saving them?"

"No, sir. All were killed outright. Dead by the time I got to them."

I studied his eyes. What secrets were locked behind them?

"Well, that's four less VC I guess," I said. "Poor bastards, hope it was quick."

"I hope it hurt," he rejoined.

Three days later I transferred Shives to the Ranger Company. We both concluded he would do better as a ranger than as a medic. He was no longer fit to be a medic. He had become even more vicious a killer than the rest of us, and for him it was unforgivable. The war was bad enough. I could not tolerate it getting any worse.

At the end of the morning's fight, we linked up with the rest of the company, essentially a reinforced platoon that had comprised the blocking force. I turned over our prisoners to the platoon leader, a youngster on his first action who, I later found out, did not last another two weeks. Predictably, the company commander had stayed back at the company base.

"Bring the gooks over to the CP," the lieutenant postured to my sergeant.

"They aren't gooks," I said quietly. "They're soldiers, just like you and me."

For a moment I thought I saw Killigan's eyes flash, then we started our journey home.

# CHAPTER 20

# THE ORDER

The army does its business by doctrine. Basic rules of tactics are established, and units at all levels adhere to them. It is a highly efficient means of applying a common style across theaters, continents, and hemispheres, so that any U.S. Army unit from anywhere in the world can be placed alongside any other U.S. Army unit elsewhere in the world and instantly be speaking a common tactical language. However, it also lays out for a smart enemy an unvarying way of doing things, allowing inherent vulnerabilities to become apparent and exploited. The Viet Cong and the North Vietnamese were smart enemies.

In our sector, they had discovered the imaginary lines dividing one unit's area of operations from another's. Because we were wary of running into another unit's ambushes and patrols—into friendly fire—we created a sort of no-man's land between ourselves and the adjacent unit. Once the enemy observed our avoidance of the creases between the areas of operations, they used them as routes of movement. Our plan, therefore, was to deny them this sanctuary.

At that time our company commander's tour in the field was coming to an end. Given the man's personal timidity and ineptness at company-level tactics, that should have been bad news for the enemy. But with an eye toward the inevitable efficiency report that determines an officer's measure of success or failure during a tour of duty, the outgoing commander planned one final company-level operation before he left the field.

Accordingly, at noon one bright, sunny day I received a call on the platoon radio to patrol up to 3d Platoon, some three thousand meters to my north-northwest. The commander would meet me there with the other two rifle platoon leaders to give the company operations order.

Sergeant James and three of his men would take me and my RTO to the linkup. I made two key changes in the squad before starting out: Phil Nail became my RTO once again, and Killigan joined James's squad in his old position as point man. Killigan had been constantly haranguing me to let him do what he did best, and I finally yielded. Barely suppressing a smile that rearranged his classically stoic face, Killigan passed the radio and code books to Nail and got ready to move out. He was going "home," back up to point.

Our course took us to the west, and then north. Killigan lived up to his reputation, steering clear of two booby traps awaiting our journey. At a point fifteen hundred meters northwest of our platoon perimeter, he led us across a briskly moving stream and immediately picked up a trail heading due north. Trusting to the safety of the trail for only a few meters, we left it as soon as possible for some solid ground away from the rice paddies that permeated the area.

As we entered 3d Platoon's perimeter, I spied Captain Moray, the young company commander, standing with the two other platoon leaders. Moray looked clean and rested, too clean and rested. He was about my age, a graduate from West Point one year before me. In those days rank could be made quickly: first lieutenant after one year, captain after the second. In a year I would have Moray's rank, but I hoped I wouldn't show my inexperience as glaringly as he did.

"Lieutenant McDonough reporting as ordered, sir." I

saluted with my right hand, my left hand balancing my rifle on my left hip, the barrel pointing toward the ground.

"Hello, Jim." Captain Moray gave me a broad smile. I nodded to the two lieutenants. They were new to me. The turnover rate among lieutenants in the company and battalion was enormously high. For a long time I had been the senior surviving rifle platoon leader in the company, and—although I couldn't be sure of it— probably in the battalion as well.

"This is the plan, gentlemen," Moray proceeded. "Second and Third Platoons will link up during hours of darkness tonight and then conduct a search-and-destroy operation into Alpha Company's area of operations to the west. First Platoon will constitute the company reserve and remain at its platoon perimeter. Company mortars will provide fire support."

"Where will you be, sir?" I asked, although I already knew the answer.

"I'll be with 1st Platoon. That's the best way I can control the fire support and movement of the reserve— as well as have access to the radios with battalion and Alpha Company." Moray laid his excuses out carefully.

The plan would put Moray two thousand meters away from our present location, and four thousand meters away from the objective. I tried to conceal my disdain.

"Sir, request permission to control the operational movement of maneuver forces in the initial phase of the operation." I spoke with what I hoped was a totally expressionless face.

"Sure, Jim, I guess that makes sense. You're the senior lieutenant among the platoons. Did you have a plan in mind?" Moray was easy, and I was going to take advantage of it.

I briefed him on my concept—routes of movement, where we would set up, time of anticipated contact with the enemy, and types of weaponry we would carry. The captain concurred with the plans, then excused himself. "I've got to get back to the CP and report to battalion."

Seeing an opportunity for complete freedom of action, I continued. "Sir, I need to flesh out the details with the other platoon leaders. May I brief them in your absence?"

"Yes, certainly. Carry on." He left as we stood up to salute.

I tried to preserve Moray's objective, which was to deter free and open movement by the enemy down the units' dividing line, while making the tactics less susceptible to blunder. I knew that a midnight linkup of two keyed-up platoons was a form of suicide, so I instructed 3d Platoon to stay put. Meanwhile I would feign a patrol in my own sector in order to throw the enemy off and then move up to 3d Platoon's location and continue on to the objective area. However, I could see no need for a two-platoon force sneaking into unfamiliar territory in the dark, so I asked the platoon lieutenant to give me only his best point man as a guide through 3d Platoon's sector into the neighboring company's area of operations.

The platoon leader, Lieutenant Smalley, agreed. He had been in the field only a month and did not seem to be properly cast for his job. The son of middle-class Bostonians from Roxbury, he was out of place as an infantry platoon leader. Perhaps he would have avoided the war if he had had the connections of some of his Cambridge neighbors. Instead he opted to turn his college ROTC experience into a two-year hitch as an officer, thereby avoiding the draft and enlisted service. Slight and withdrawn, he was uncomfortable with the business of leadership.

A glance around the platoon perimeter warned me not to depend too much on Smalley's platoon coming through in a pinch. The whole position seemed disheveled, unmilitary, as if all efforts had been expended for comfort rather than for tactical prudence. No defensive field of fire had been cleared, and I could see brush growing right up to the flimsy barbed wire encircling the position. The unit was situated in a cluster of rubbled buildings, apparently a destroyed monastery. The soldiers had strung hammocks under taut ponchos stretched over the half-demolished walls. Garbage was everywhere, a sure sign of a poorly disciplined unit. As we spoke, I could hear music blaring from transistor radios tuned to the Armed Forces Network. Where I could distinguish fighting positions, they seemed badly located and without adequate cover.

Even more significantly, I spied two young women within the perimeter. They had set up a brothel inside one of the wrecked buildings, and while the unit officers spoke, the women were turning a profit from the visiting patrols. Apparently the brothel had been operating for some time, judging by the jealous looks on the faces of the 3d Platoon soldiers, who did not like "their women" bestowing favors on outsiders. Observing all this, I silently wrote Lieutenant Smalley out of the plan. If he could not exercise minimum control in the defense, he would surely fall apart in the attack.

Lieutenant Evans, 1st Platoon's leader, was anxious. He had been on the job only a week and this was his first operation. He was a tall, good-looking boy from the Midwest, but I felt he was too eager. He was disappointed to be standing pat for the night as the reserve unit, but the call had been Moray's, not mine.

Perhaps it was unfair of me to make snap judgments of others and then plan my actions on the basis of those judgments. The thought bothered me, but not enough to deter me. I was in the business of evaluating people, and the traits of other men would determine my own fate and that of my soldiers. Presumptuous though my role may have been, I had to make judgments and act accordingly.

Moray was timid, Smalley was weak, Evans was eager. I did not condemn them for that. I noted it and adjusted. We were in a war, not a community social.

# CHAPTER 21

# THE PATROL BACK

"Okay, Sergeant James, get the men ready to move out," I called as I folded up my map.

Private James Taylor from Baltimore, Maryland, shot me a look of dismay. He was next in line to see one of the girls. "Hey, sir, what's the hurry? Can't we set up about ten more minutes?"

"Come on, Taylor, we've got a whole platoon waiting for the word about tonight. I'm doing you a favor stopping you short of the 'rest' you have in mind." I chuckled inwardly at his predicament.

Taylor, one of three black soldiers in the platoon, was a first-rate rifleman. Well over six feet tall, he had suffered the fate of many big men in Vietnam: he was an easy target; he had already been wounded twice. But he kept coming back. I think it was his appreciation of the needs of his friends, black and white, that did it.

Killigan led us out through the wire. The sun was beating down on our backs as we made our way south. I kept mulling over the plan for the night. Sergeant James, right behind Killigan, was directing his movement, taking care to steer clear of the route we had taken on the way north. It was shortly past 1500, and there was much to do before moving out on the operation after dark. We were trying to move fast.

As we neared the stream we had crossed earlier in the day, the terrain became increasingly restrictive. To our west, a north-south rice paddy some fifty meters in width forced us up against dense vegetation that slowed our movement. A narrow trail threaded in a southerly direction between the paddy and the vegetation, but it was a trail we had used briefly on the way up, so we avoided it for as long as possible.

About fifty meters short of the ford of the stream Killigan doglegged to the west and brought us up on the trail. The heavy labor in the brush brought beads of sweat to my forehead, and I concentrated on our present movement, leaving thoughts of the night operation for later. We were soon in the treacherous position of doubling back on a previously used route, always a dangerous tactic. For a second, I considered yelling at Killigan to get off the trail, but we were so close to the ford that by the time we maneuvered off the trail, we would be at the crossing site.

As Killigan moved ahead in his stealthy glide, I saw him freeze momentarily and then glance to his left directly into a bush overlooking the trail. I knew in an instant that we were in imminent danger, for Killigan never made abrupt moves except at the moment of conflict. Killigan turned back to us, his face contorting as if to shout a warning. I yelled "Ambush" and dove to my left. Killigan took a grenade blast full in the face at point-blank range. At the same time, Sergeant James went down with a bullet in his shoulder. The enemy was spraying us from a position across the rice paddy. Killigan had hit a command-detonated booby trap.

I pressed my face into the dirt as bullets whined over my outstretched body. I calculated that at best only four of us were left. I peeked out from under my helmet to see James struggling to get off the trail, the red blotch widening on his dark green fatigues. He was moving not into the bushes, but toward Killigan, who was lying facedown in the paddy where the blast had knocked him, his blood turning the yellowish water red. Within minutes, if he were still alive, Killigan would drown.

"Put out a base of fire," I shouted to the three men strung out behind me. They all responded as James slid into the water to grab Killigan. I fired a clip from my M-16 and dashed to James's side, standing waist-deep in the paddy water, the ooze beneath sucking at my boots. Together we pulled Killigan from the water. James's arm was shattered, so it was up to me to drag Killigan across the trail and behind a dirt mound where I could work on him. James propped his rifle on the mound and added to the fire of the other three men, painstakingly working the weapon with his one good arm.

Killigan was alive but bleeding profusely from holes throughout his body, starting at the right temple and pocking down his neck, torso, and legs to a point just above the knees. I worked furiously to rip his clothes away so I could get at the wounds, but the soggy material, saturated by water and blood, withstood my efforts. Killigan, tough as ever, was still conscious; unable to speak because of mouth and throat wounds, he motioned to his right trouser pocket. There I found a highly sharpened pocketknife and proceeded to slice through the fatigues.

As I worked, Nail crawled up to me with the radio. "Shit, L.T., we're in a world of hurt now! How's Killigan?"

"This tough bastard is just fine," I lied. "Call the CO and tell him our situation." The exchange of fire was now barking back and forth. Once again, time was our ally: the more we had, the better our chances of overcoming the enemy. But Killigan did not have much time.

As Captain Moray ordered Lieutenant Evans's 1st Platoon to push out from the north, I ordered Platoon Sergeant Palloman to take the rest of my platoon, minus three men to hold the perimeter, and sweep in from the south. I knew Palloman could move fast, while Lieutenant Evans had to link up with his own platoon before coming to our rescue. Characteristically, Captain Moray elected to stay back at the command post.

Nail continued his vital mission on the radio, our link to salvation, and called for a medevac for Killigan and James; Pfc Taylor kept pumping out M-79 rounds on the enemy ambush position across the rice paddy. By making it a far ambush, the enemy had given us a chance. They couldn't rush across the paddy. They had banked everything on tripping the booby trap and cutting us down as we stood in line. I sensed that my boxer's reflexes had saved me and the trailing men from that fate, but it was Killigan's sacrifice, turning to warn us before saving himself, that gave us the split second to get down.

Killigan was going to die if he didn't receive prompt medical attention. My first aid was not enough, and I continually had to interrupt my work to return fire at the enemy. Moray had ordered me to fix the enemy in place, and I tried to do that, but there were only four of us able to shoot. So far, I had discovered seventeen wounds in Killigan's body including three in the head, one in the throat, two in the chest, three in the abdomen, and one in the groin. His eyes were rolling up under his lids as if he were falling away into a deep sleep—or death.

"Hang on, buddy, I'll get you out of here." I made my commitment softly. His watery eyes floated down from their hiding place and fixed on me for a second. It was a glimpse into eternity. I would not let him die. I would rip the world off its axis first.

As he drifted back into his daze, the chopping sound of the helicopter's blades roared into earshot. The pilot's voice crackled over the radio. "This is Casper Four-Niner. Pop smoke."

Nail threw out a red smoke grenade.

"Got it. Ruby red," the pilot chattered.

"Affirmative," Nail answered, the bullets chewing up the ground around him.

"Give me an LZ and I'll come in." Casper Four-Nine was asking a lot, but he had to have a place to land.

Our immediate location was too thickly vegetated to bring in the Huey helicopter, but thirty meters at our rear to the east, the trees and bushes thinned enough to allow the aircraft to hover.

"Give me a max rate of fire," I shouted to the squad. "Nail, move to that clearing and pop smoke, then get back here and cover!"

I turned to Killigan and picked him up in my arms, cradling him like a baby. The rifle strapped over my neck and shoulder sawed into my neck. Killigan and I each weighed in at about one hundred fifty pounds— this was going to be the longest journey of my life. Step-by-step I struggled through the undergrowth toward the green smoke billowing up in the clearing. My arms shook from the effort, sending painful tremors through Killigan's body, and he clenched his teeth with each jerky movement. He would have fainted had he been a weaker man. His blood dripped through my hands; it ran in rivulets through the creases of my bent arms.

James took my weapon from around my neck, afraid I would strangle from the constriction across my throat. He carried his own and Killigan's equipment. The sergeant had yet to tend to his own wound.

I lurched for ten meters, bullets whacking into trees on either side of me. The world was spinning. Sweat cascaded down my forehead into my eyes. My chest was crushed by my own exertion, and I couldn't breathe.

Nail ran past me back to his post. Killigan struggled to stay conscious.

The second ten meters were agonizing. James kept encouraging Killigan and me. I wished I were a bigger man. I leaned against a tree as I saw the helicopter descending into the clearing. With a burst of energy I staggered toward it.

As I made it to the LZ the helicopter hovered at chest level, the pilot's face frozen with fear. He had just realized that rounds were impacting all over the place. The door gunner opened with his M-60 machine gun over our heads.

As I struggled to lift Killigan up into the floor of the waiting craft, my strength failed just as the pilot lost his nerve. The helicopter abruptly ascended as I sank to my knees with my dying burden. Gently I laid him down; for an instant he resigned himself to death. The blood flowed from more holes than I could plug.

I would not have it. I scrambled to the radio Nail had wisely left in the clearing. "Come back down here!" I yelled into the mouthpiece.

"Negative! Negative! You've got a hot LZ down there!"

"Get down here, you yellow son of a bitch or I'll shoot you down!" My radio procedure fell by the wayside.

"Look," I settled down, "I'll secure this LZ if you come in." I tried to avoid pleading.

I dashed back to the rice paddy, dragging my M-16 as I ran. The helicopter hesitated and began its descent. I fired my weapon on full automatic, inserted another magazine, and sprayed again.

"Shoot it up!" I called to the three remaining men of the patrol. As I ran back to Killigan a furious fire rose from our guns.

I picked up Killigan; his eyes were shut. The helicopter hovered within reach. "Fire that machine gun!" I yelled to the door gunner. His eyes wide with fear, the gunner ripped the belt of 7.62-millimeter rounds through the chamber, a scythe of lead emitting from the barrel.

I tried to hoist Killigan from my waist to my shoulders. I couldn't do it. Grunting and cursing, I looked at the pilot's panic-stricken face. It was do or die; in an instant Killigan would be gone. My strength failed me, my arms were weakening; then Killigan opened his eyes. He stretched his arms out to the helicopter skid and did a chin-up. Amazed, I grabbed his feet and heaved him onto the floor of the helicopter. In the next instant, Sergeant James, upon my order, scrambled aboard the medevac and the helicopter was gone.

Only four of us remained on the ground, but as I grabbed the radio and my weapon and made my way back to the rice paddy, I knew the tide had turned. Killigan made it out because he refused to die. I would beat back the enemy because I refused to be beaten. Much of life is a matter of will, and so is war. As long as breath remains, there is hope.

Sergeant Palloman was closing in from the south by that time. Lieutenant Evans and his platoon had already crossed the rice paddy to the north and were turning south. The plan was to close in on the enemy from two flanks while keeping them engaged to the front. They must have gotten the picture, for they abruptly tried to break contact. I couldn't call in artillery or mortar fire because we were working in a populated area, and clearance would have taken too long. The only option was to keep the pressure on by pursuit.

Fifty meters across a rice paddy is a long march. It is like walking through a minefield. At any moment the enemy may open up on you and tear your unit apart. The muck grabs at your legs. You can't make speed in any direction once the journey has begun. There is no place to hide. There is only the brush at the end of the paddy, behind which the enemy can choose the time and place to strike. You move with a fixed stare on the line of foliage, hoping to catch a glimpse of movement a second before the shooting starts. The four of us walking in line felt like so many ducks in a shooting gallery. It was amazing that the other three men even followed my orders to move forward. But they did. They always did.

Sergeant Palloman was making good time closing in from the south. I could hear small arms fire coming from his position, and as we crashed through the brush beyond the rice paddy we caught a glimpse of the fleeing enemy. He was starting to take casualties, and unlike us he had no medical evacuation helicopter to fly them out.

First Platoon, coming in from the north, reported sighting a small enemy group moving in toward the battle. On that report, I ordered my men to set up a hasty ambush. Luck ran with the enemy, however, as the first ones into our kill zone were a farmer and two water buffalo. The latter caught wind of the four of us in the bushes and gave us away. I waved the farmer on. But I knew our position was too compromised to dally there any longer.

I swung south and linked up with the rest of my platoon. Sergeant Palloman sadly pointed out to me that among the casualties was a young Vietnamese farm girl. Apparently she had been tending a water buffalo in the field and had taken a round in the neck as the battle raged by her. I didn't know who hit her; it could have been us or the enemy. There was no telling from the wound, a gaping hole that had torn out the left side of her throat. Even though her corpse was a gory sight, it was obvious that she had been a beautiful girl and very young.

For the most part, the fight had ended. When Lieutenant Evans and his platoon came in from the north to join us, he reported that the enemy had effectively broken contact. Although 1st Platoon had exchanged some fire at a distance with pockets of enemy, they had neither lost nor claimed casualties. By that time I was busy arranging for the requisite reports to be called in, preparing for the move back to my platoon position, and dispatching the other platoon back to its area of operations. There was, however, one final scene to be played out.

Lieutenant Evans had arrived with all the eagerness and naiveté of youth. He had been in his first battle and the adrenalin was coursing through his veins. "I heard you got a couple," he said. "Any of the bodies around here?"

I was repulsed by his enthusiasm. Obviously, he had not yet seen any casualties, and to him, war was still a game of good guys versus bad guys. I decided to sober him up.

"Over there in the bushes you'll find what you're looking for." I directed him toward the body of the young girl.

With an expectant grin Evans set off to gaze at the gruesome sight. I could see the back of his neck stiffen as he came upon the corpse. For a few moments he stood frozen, the hair almost bristling on the back of his head. Then he lurched to his left and vomited.

A few minutes later he returned to my position. The zeal was gone from his eyes, replaced by a mixture of revulsion and hatred. Perhaps I had played God a little too much. At that moment he and I were worlds apart. Evans might have been me when I first arrived in Vietnam, but now we were two different species.

# CHAPTER 22

# NIGHT MOVEMENT

Sergeant Palloman was hopping mad. He didn't want to stay back at the perimeter that night. He wanted to go out and get revenge for Killigan. But I needed him there. Only seven men would stay behind; the other twelve would be on the operation. Seven men to hold the perimeter through the night was less than adequate. They needed a good leader—Palloman.

We had lost two men that afternoon; I had to borrow a few from 3d Platoon. Sergeant Donne—by far the strongest squad leader—would go with me, and I would beef up his squad with the extra men. Sergeant James had been lost that afternoon, and the Spec 4 I designated to take his place was not very strong. I wanted Nail to remain my RTO; it did no good to switch radio men back and forth. I would take the same men with me who had come through the enemy ambush. They were tired, but I couldn't afford to leave a skimpy *and* tired force with Palloman. If the enemy realized how lightly the perimeter was held, they could put terrible pressure on him while I was away. I was glad I had been persistent in confounding the enemy's intelligence system. There was a chance now that I could sneak the twelve men away undetected or at the very least conceal the exact number departing.

Taylor approached me. "Let me take the point, lieutenant."

"How are you feeling, Taylor?" I asked, trying to assess his nerves.

"I'm fine. I just want to make sure we find our way back to 3d Platoon. My woman is waiting for me." He was lying. Like the rest of us, he looked up to Killigan, and now he wanted to take his place on point. It was a matter of honor.

"Okay. Get some chow. You'll need your strength for what's waiting for you." We were speaking in code to each other.

By dusk the sky was overcast, promising a dark night of covered stars and moon. We would have to stay close to each other on our journey. In accordance with our standard operating procedures, I made sure each man reviewed his actions for the night, before the sun set. I would take two radios with me and borrow two more from 3d Platoon. Communications would be a key factor in the upcoming operation.

We slipped out of the wire with full darkness at 1930. Taylor took the lead, followed by the newly appointed squad leader. Nail was third, radio firmly attached to his back. I walked fourth, trying to keep a close eye on the point man and the inexperienced squad leader. Behind me walked King, the grenadier, the soldier who had taken a shot at me when I burned his marijuana.

We zigzagged to the west. If any enemy had spotted us, I hoped we could pull them away from Palloman. Although the night was dark, control had been good. We were moving essentially without noise; there was only the occasional whisper from me to the point to shift left or right, and the intermittent passing up of the "count" from rear to front to insure no one became separated from the column. It had been a long day, but so far fatigue had been staved off. We had eaten, and the soldier often finds food a substitute for rest. We were moving well. We shifted to the north and began our journey toward 3d Platoon.

An hour out from Truong Lam we came to the edge of a rice paddy, not too far from where Killigan had been hurt earlier in the day. I wondered if he were still alive, then tried to force the thought from my mind.

The water in the paddy was exceptionally high. Once a man stepped into the ooze he was in up to his hips. Sloshing around would be a noisy affair, so I told Taylor to search for a solid dike on which to cross. The darkness would cover our silhouettes. After a few minutes, Taylor picked one out and we started across.

Halfway across the dike, there was a sudden exchange of gunfire. From my position at the near end of the dike I could only make out the muzzle flashes, see the tracers slice out into the night, and hear the squad leader cry out into the dark, "Taylor's hit!"

Taylor had come face to face with three Viet Cong crossing on the dike from the other end. Both sides had exchanged fire simultaneously, the first rounds going high as they almost always do. Taylor knew he was in a bad position, and as he emptied his magazine he turned to shout a warning back to the rest of us. At that instant he took a round in the back and spilled over into the paddy. The squad leader, second in line, jumped back to our side of the paddy. Apparently the Viet Cong also jumped back, and now we were taking fire from a line across the paddy.

"Donne, bring your squad on line and give us some fire!" I yelled above the din. I eased into the paddy, followed closely by Taylor's squad leader. Ten meters out we found the wounded point man. He was struggling to keep his head above the water, but his wound and the muck were dragging him down. I grabbed his tightly curled hair and pulled him over to hug the side of the dike from which he had fallen. The dike was perpendicular to the line of fire and did not offer us much cover. Like children futilely hiding behind bed covers, we cowered by the useless dike, noses above the water while bullets skimmed just above the paddy.

"Oh, shit! It hurts!" Taylor complained of his wound, the bleeding hole somewhere below the surface of the filthy paddy water. We were in a true standoff, neither side able to advance across the rice paddy, neither side willing to break contact and give away an advantage.

I ordered the squad leader to return to his squad and fire the LAWs I had insisted on carrying. There were no enemy tanks in that area of Vietnam, but I knew that the shock effect of the LAW was so great that it would unnerve the most resolute enemy. For two long minutes Taylor and I waited in silence. Then the LAW screamed overhead and exploded on the enemy shore in blinding roars. The enemy broke contact.

"Donne, get your squad after them," I yelled back over Taylor's head. As Donne and his men swept by me, I dragged the wounded man back to dry land. The medic took over as I went to join Sergeant Donne. A real professional, he had kept his squad on line and was beating the enemy back into the bush. Donne's large frame drove the line of American soldiers before him as calmly as if they were picking cotton. After a hundred meters I stopped him. We still had a night's mission ahead of us, and we had to get Taylor out. We fell back and secured a landing zone while Nail called for a medevac.

Taylor was in amazingly good spirits. In a perverse sort of way, luck had been with him. The bullet that hit him had gone through four magazines in the pouch he wore on his web belt, the web belt itself, and his flak jacket. Although the bullet ripped into him deeply, it didn't exit his body. An exit wound from a shot fired at that range would have been devastating.

"I got me a million-dollar wound, Lieutenant Mac," Taylor gloated, his white teeth flashing in the glimmer from the light the medic held as he probed at the wound. But the terrible shakes I had seen come over so many wounded men, and had suffered myself when hit, belied his outward calm.

Taylor had been lucky, but all bets weren't in yet. The medevac helicopter had to make it in in the dark, an infinitely more difficult feat than Killigan's evacuation earlier that day. The enemy had pulled back, but they were still out there in the darkness, sure to be drawn by the helicopter's searchlight as it tried to find the ground in the dark.

Cautiously I drew the platoon into a ring and began to push the men out around the landing zone we had prepared. Taylor was waiting patiently, but his face showed his pain.

From the distance came the first faint sounds of helicopter rotors. I pushed the men out another ten meters as I fired a red flare from the center of the ring.

Fortunately I had carried a strobe light on the mission and I drew in the helicopter with its flickering light, the pilot and I talking to each other steadily as he approached our position. At the last moment the enemy tried to foil the rescue by opening fire on the descending helicopter, but we were ready. Our return fire drove them back. In an instant, Taylor was aboard and gone. We never saw him again and chose to believe he truly did receive "the million-dollar wound."

With Taylor gone, several men volunteered to take the point. I chose one and we moved out: the point man, the squad leader, Nhan, myself, Nail, and the rest of the patrol behind us.

At 2200 our route took us into a stream that meandered slowly to the north. Despite the chilly chest-high water, we made better time and less noise moving with the flow of the river. Holding our weapons above our heads, we tightened up the column and continued our movement toward our interim destination, 3d Platoon.

Our movement didn't go well. The river bed fell away in places and soldiers suddenly found themselves in over their heads. Although it was only a few feet to firmer footing, the men hesitated, sometimes even balked, at moving forward. I went up and down the line encouraging and cajoling them to move forward, but our progress was slow.

Things got worse before they got better. At 2300 the count passed up to me was "one," meaning only five of us were present counting the three in front of me. The tail end of the patrol had become disconnected in the dark; somewhere in the river, six men were lost. Leaders aren't supposed to try to be heroes. They don't walk on point because the point man is the most exposed and therefore the most expendable man in the unit. By definition, the leader is the least expendable, yet there are times when the leader can ask no one else to do what must be done. Finding the rest of the patrol in the dark was my job. Radio contact could not be made, probably because of the wet handsets. I would have to grope for the men, and they were no doubt tense, aware they were cut off in the dark, nervous fingers on triggers.

Before I began my journey back upstream I put the four remaining men in ambush position beside the stream. Their instructions were to continue on to 3d Platoon if I didn't return within an hour.

I was nervous. Alone in the water, I felt exposed on all sides. The enemy couldn't be far away. My own men might have moved off astride the stream and set up an ambush. Or I might meet them coming down the stream, much as Taylor had bumped into the Viet Cong a short while ago. I worried that the night's operation might go

wrong, and the failure would be my fault. The clammy
fatigues stuck to my skin, and my heart thumped in my
chest. The load on my shoulders and back threatened to
press me down under the black water. Once again, I was
fighting to control my personal fears and meet my responsibilities to my men and to the mission.

Up ahead in the water was a small darkness a shade
blacker than the darkness around it. Silently I approached as close as I could without being heard, until
I knew that an inch more would cause it to react.

"King, is that you?" I called softly. What I would
do if it wasn't, I had no idea.

"Lieutenant?" The voice bordered on panic.

"Easy, King. It's me. Just take it easy now." My
own voice quivered.

We touched in the darkness, peering into each
other's face: King, the man who had once fired at me,
and I, the man who had once held a rifle to his head. We
were overjoyed to see each other. All six of the men
were there. We tightened up the column and returned to
the front half of the patrol. Reunited, we left the stream
and continued on our way to our sister platoon.

We were close to it. Nail had disassembled his radio
in the dark and dried the pieces and was trying to raise
3d Platoon. There was no answer. We made a radio
check back to Sergeant Palloman. His voice came back
loud and clear. Our radio was working, but no answer
came from 3d Platoon despite repeated calls.

Five hundred meters beyond the stream I halted the
patrol. Even in the dark I sensed that we were right on
top of 3d Platoon. We had to make radio contact before
we proceeded.

Third Platoon still didn't answer. In desperation we
radioed to company headquarters, who in turn tried to
raise the platoon. Nothing. For thirty minutes, the futile
radio calls went out.

We couldn't sit there all night. We were in a precarious position, and staying where we were would not accomplish the mission. I estimated we were within direct-fire range of 3d Platoon. To move in on them unannounced was to risk startling them into firing at us. Although the platoon knew we were coming, I knew that the men on the perimeter would shoot first and ask questions later. I had no faith in 3d Platoon's leadership, and the lack of radio response confirmed my earlier doubts. But there was no way around the situation. We would proceed to a physical linkup, unannounced. For the second time that night I took up the point position. I could allow no one else to do it.

Fifty meters from our starting position my foot triggered a trip flare. The brightly burning candle illuminated me against the background of the underbrush. A machine gun barrel directly to my front swung around to lock in on my chest. The patrol behind me fell to the ground, bracing for the onslaught of fire. I stood stock-still calling out as loudly as I could, my heart wedged in my mouth: "Don't shoot!" I knew that if I too dove to the ground it would precipitate a firefight.

Sergeant Donne appeared next to me in the glare of the burning flare, his moves purposeful and authoritative. "Hold your fire, you assholes!"

With his bulky frame and bellowing voice, Donne could not be mistaken for a Vietnamese. The big man had come forward to share the risk of being instantly cut down. Within a heartbeat, the machine gunner decided not to fire. Amid curses from the men on the perimeter at our stupidity for sneaking up on them in the dark, we entered into 3d Platoon.

I thanked Donne and went immediately to find Smalley, the 3d Platoon leader (asleep), and his RTO (also asleep). Barely controlling my rage, I let Smalley know what I thought of his leadership. He protested that he and his men were exhausted by the activities of the day. I glowered; he got no sympathy from me.

There was nothing to be gained by anger, so I put it aside and laid out the plans for the night. I would take four men from 3d Platoon, including one on point, and leave at 0400. After moving into the edge of the next company's area of operations, I would set up a series of premorning ambushes. I then lay down on my gear for two hours rest. Sleep came instantly but not deeply: there were too many responsibilities weighing on my mind.

It is morning, and there is a grimness in the drizzly air. Silent figures move to the west, shoulders bent under equipment loads, buckles taped for silence, camouflage paint smeared on taut faces. Ghouls in the night—young boys, really, from places like Valdosta, San Diego, Boulder, Madison, Portland, out to kill Asian boys who are out to kill them. The gears of war grind together unrelentingly, mechanisms in motion that will catch up human flesh as they mesh. Societies clash, politicians deal, diplomats debate, young men struggle to the death. Tomorrow or the next day, mothers will receive the news and cry. But nothing will stop the morning's killing.

By 0530 we set up four ambush points each about one hundred meters apart—three groups of four and one group of three. Together they comprise an area ambush along the interlocking trail network. I put myself with Nail and Nhan and a borrowed soldier. Quietly we belly up to a clump of bushes beside the trail. The waiting begins. As we lie on the wet, lush earth, I wonder how my wife is. I long to be home.

The minutes tick away. Our eyes become heavy. How can men sleep in such circumstances? Danger cannot keep

us alert. Danger is always present; there is nothing excep-
tional about it. We accept it. We blot it out. Sleep is a
more elementary need. It tries to consume us. We fight to
stay awake.

The drizzle ends. Slowly, the sky begins to lighten,
almost imperceptibly at first. We can see a few meters to
our front. The 3d Platoon soldier crawls away to answer the call of nature. Nail works at his radio; the
dampness has rendered it inoperable again. Nhan, forty
years old and weary, has drifted off to sleep. I wonder
how the other ambush positions are doing and crawl
over to Nail to help him with the radio.

At that moment the enemy walks through our ambush position. We can do nothing. No one is poised to
shoot. Three Viet Cong are blissfully unaware that they
have flirted with death and escaped. They are proceeding toward the next position. Frantically, we reassemble
the radio and whisper a warning over the airwaves. Simultaneously, another group of enemy walks into the
third ambush site. It is tripped and all the enemy are
killed; the first group of three hears the melee and pan-
ics. One darts back. Nhan, the old scout, catches him
with a round in the side. He falls and the old man fin-
ishes him with two more in the head. Two of the enemy
scramble through Sergeant Donne's position and are hit.
One falls dead. The other scampers into the brush.
Donne pursues. The wounded enemy ducks into a hole
in the ground. Obviously he is familiar with the territory. In Vietnamese, Donne yells for him to come out.
There is no reply. Donne yells again. Bullets spray out of
the hole. Donne lobs in a grenade. Dirt, leaves, and flesh
fly out of the opening in front of the blast. Donne throws
in a second grenade. A death rattle rasps from the hole.

Sergeant Donne looks around for the newest soldier. Spotting an eighteen-year-old, he sends him in: a
safe way to harden the youngster toward the events in

store for him during the year to come. The youth emerges, dragging the Viet Cong behind him. It's a gruesome sight. The man's face—nose, mouth, eyes—is gone. Air is sucked in and out of the hole where the nostrils used to connect, the jelly-like mess rising and falling in bubbles. Wounds gape everywhere on his body. There is nothing we can do for him. It would be inhumane to prolong his agony.

The mission is over now. After all the shooting it would be pointless to stay in the ambush positions. I am worried about the handful of Americans left at Truong Lam. With daylight upon us, it might become apparent that only seven men are there. We set course for 3d Platoon and drop off the four borrowed men. Setting an azimuth to the south-southeast, thereby avoiding areas we had crossed over in the past twenty-four hours, we begin our journey home.

Home—that is what our platoon perimeter is to us. Its comforts are few, but it is where we feel most comfortable. It may be the most contested acreage in that section of Vietnam, but it is where we feel most secure. It is our platoon perimeter, and we are a unit woven together by our shared experiences. We almost yearn to get back.

The enemy is not done with us yet. It has been a bloody twenty-four hours for them also, and they must seek their revenge as we have sought ours. A VC squad lies in wait to our front and greets us with a quick volley of fire as we emerge into a clearing. The rounds go high. They are tired, as are we, and they don't have the stomach to prolong the fight. They withdraw. My bloodlust is up, and we pursue.

I am a boxer again. I sense my opponent is reeling. I have lost three men since yesterday, but he has lost several times that many. That last outburst was a futile jab launched in anger and desperation, but essentially to cover a retreat. I can sense a knockout. Put him away. Don't let him fight another day. But we are hurt, too. How long can we continue? Finish it now. Close in and end it once and for all. I charge in, driving the men before me as if they were an extension of my own body, tired and hurt but keyed for the kill.

We chase fleeting targets for two hundred meters. Suddenly a cluster of huts appears to our front. It could be the showdown. I put five men on line to provide cover and take the other five on a rush toward the huts. Sweeping around the corner of the first building we spy a group of Vietnamese standing in a common area amid the huts. A few meters away stands a lone male beside a chest-high rice urn. He is tall and thin, perhaps eighteen years of age. I focus on him. His movements are suspicious. We yell for everyone to freeze. All comply, but the tall young male makes a sudden lurching movement toward the urn. Still on the run, I tighten my finger on the trigger. When we are only a few feet apart I whip the rifle barrel alongside his face and knock him to the ground. I stand over him, poised for the kill, the barrel of my rifle pointing directly at his chest. My eyes search for the weapon he must have pulled from the urn. I want to spot it so I can fall away from its business end as I kill him. I see nothing.

A woman from the group falls to her knees. In Vietnamese she pleads with me to spare her son. I look at her as she begins to crawl through the dirt toward me, bawling as she comes. She has seen the look on my face. She knows I mean to kill.

I turn back to the boy. His arms and legs are jerking. He is trying to get up but has no control over his muscles. A confused smile is on his face, and the welt from the rifle barrel is reddening. He is a spastic. His lurch toward the urn was only his inability to walk smoothly. Even as I stand over him, his mother crawls on top of him, shielding his body with her own.

Revulsion hits me like a shot. I feel ashamed and sick to my stomach. I bend over and try to pull the woman to her feet, asking in English for her forgiveness. Her terror only increases; she doesn't know what to make of this madman hovering over her. I pat her head. As she realizes that the danger is passed, she rises from her son. A smile of relief spreads over her reddened gums.

I turn to the boy and wipe the blood from his cheek. Sheepishly, I brush at the dirt on his black pajamas. His smiles cuts me to the heart. I cannot believe how close I came to killing the boy, a cripple, in the presence of his family. Only chance spared him. I was on a rampage. Only the shortness of the distance between us caused me to hit him rather than shoot him.

I knew that killing him would have been neither illegal nor immoral. It would have been "regrettable," but nothing more. In an instant the insanity of war was revealed to me: people die or people live without rhyme or reason. As Nail had said when Fricker died: "That's all there is to it."

The operation was over. I gathered in my forces and marched back to Truong Lam. There had been enough killing for one day. Tomorrow it would start again, but for today I wanted to be alone with my thoughts. Somehow I had to try to understand the meaning of it all.

# CHAPTER 23

# END OF A MISSION

My time in the field was drawing to a close. The practice in Vietnam, criticized by all, was for officers to rotate out of the field to another job after approximately half of their tour. I had already been asked to consider two jobs on the battalion staff, but I couldn't accept them as long as the option was mine. I knew that the men in my platoon were there for a full twelve months or until incapacitated by wounds, illness, or death, whichever came first. To leave them for a relatively safe job at the battalion base camp would have been, to my mind, the height of hypocrisy. A leader does not leave his men.

But the custom had been fixed long ago, beginning with the first entry of American combat forces into Vietnam. The motive must have been to insure proper exposure of all military leaders to the only war the Americans had been involved in since Korea. Exposing military leaders to the experience of battle is not an improper objective of an army seeking to improve effectiveness. However, the six-month rotation of officers was predicated on the assumption that Vietnam would be a short war. As it turned out, it was hardly that. It became in fact the longest war in the history of our nation. But once a bureaucracy as large as the U.S. Army sets a rule in place, it is almost beyond the power of mortal man to change it.

I was the most battle-experienced platoon leader in the battalion by that time, perhaps in the entire brigade. The attrition rate among lieutenants was just too high to give many a chance to compete. Longevity, and the fact that Truong Lam was an immediate challenge to the Viet Cong, gave me the edge on experience in combat. Like almost everything in the war, that fact had little to do with anything other than coincidence.

Throughout early December I ignored hints that it was time to let another lieutenant try his luck. With the company commander leaving, I could argue that I should hang on a little longer. But the bidding was going higher. The commanding general of the brigade had been passed my name as a replacement for his aide-de-camp, and he expressed an interest. Generals like to have junior grade officers of recent front-line experience close to them. It provides them with a perspective on what the troops in the trenches are thinking. I fit the bill and had been asked. There wasn't much option to the offer. I bought a little more time because the present aide was not yet ready to rotate home.

On Christmas morning I gathered up the soldiers of the platoon to mark the day. A truce had been in effect since midnight, and I planned no patrols for the duration of the cease-fire. As I glanced at the young but strained faces before me, I realized how many of the men who had given thanks with me at Thanksgiving were no longer present. Almost none of those missing had rotated home upon completion of a tour. Besides Killigan, Taylor, and James, three others had been wounded. Two had been killed. The attrition continued.

As the men squatted, sat or hunkered down behind various forms of cover, I expressed my best wishes for their good fortune in the days ahead, for the peace and security of their loved ones back home, and for God's blessing on all of them on the birthday of his Son. These were the traditional words of Christmas, but how un-Christmaslike it seemed! I avoided memories of better ones. Not forgetting the practicalities of the moment, I reminded the men that the terms of the twenty-four-hour Christmas truce allowed us to shoot back if fired upon. I then admonished them to get as much rest as possible because tomorrow we would have to work double-time to make up for all the maneuvering the enemy was doing under cover of the truce.

I was wrong. The enemy had no intention of marking Christmas Day with anything but their guns. As Sergeant Palloman and I broke open our C rations at 11 A.M. for a combined effort toward a Christmas stew, the first of five mortar attacks began falling in and around our position. The fire was desultory, however, and other than forcing us into the cover of our bunker lines as we tried to pinpoint the location of the enemy mortars, it caused little damage. While Sergeant Palloman cooked the stew, I took a squad on a flanking movement in the general direction of the source of the harassment, and forced the enemy to break contact.

Later in the afternoon, Palloman took out another squad while I rested after a surprisingly tasty meal. Even if the enemy would not cooperate, we would try to make the most of our theoretical day of rest.

By late afternoon we had undergone our third and fourth barrages, and the pretense of peace-on-earth was wearing thin. To make matters even worse, company headquarters radioed us that they had come under fire from an enemy squad, which was now withdrawing to the south. My orders were to try to intercept them.

With a reinforced squad I moved out to the north and set up a hasty ambush. The enemy squad never showed up, however, and with only ninety minutes of daylight left, we pulled out and started our patrol back, sweeping wide to the west to avoid retracing our earlier steps.

Coming to a stream with an earthen bridge over it, we decided to cross dry. We were determined to keep some semblance of Christmas in the day, and the fact that two peasants working a nearby field had just crossed the bridge testified that it was not booby-trapped. Nonetheless, we crossed it gingerly, making all the necessary tactical safeguards. One could not be too careful.

As the last man crossed, a Viet Cong popped up from beneath the water, raised an AK-47, and fired off a burst. The rounds went wide as the American, walking backwards as was the custom when crossing such danger points, fired his own M-16 at the VC. His rounds also went wide, and the enemy submerged unhurt beneath the surface of the murky water.

We were amazed. It was like fighting a human submarine. Where he had come from and where he planned on going, we had no idea. But it was obvious he had some plan of escape. I leaped into the water and found myself standing chest-deep in the slowly moving stream. Unable to fire without holding my rifle over my head and seeing nothing to fire at anyway, I did the logical thing (or so it seemed at the moment): I tossed a hand grenade a few feet from me at the place where our adversary had disappeared. Nothing happened. The grenade did not explode, so I tossed another. When they both went off, a large tree toppled from the nearby bank and almost clobbered me. The scene had the potential of being comical until the Viet Cong bobbed up to the surface. He was dead as the proverbial mackerel, his brain ruptured by the concussion. There was not a mark on his body, just a grotesque blueness to his face.

A search by one of the soldiers disclosed a subsurface entrance to a hollowed-out hole above the water line in the bank of the stream. In it our worthy opponent had slung a hammock barely above the water's surface, fitted a few candles into the wall, and hung his weapons and ammunition to keep dry. I could only marvel at his toughness and dedication. With some respect, we carried him back to the village of Truong Lam so that he might receive a proper burial by some of his countrymen.

During the evening hours we sustained two more mortar attacks. By almost all accounts, it had not been a good Christmas, but at least we had suffered no casualties. Shortly after midnight, the first patrol of the post–cease-fire went out.

It was clear that the enemy was building for another push in our area. Intelligence told us to expect more heavy action from a company or two of Viet Cong strengthened with North Vietnamese regulars. There could be no reinforcement of our platoon, however, because enemy pressure was building throughout the area. Already the battalion reconnaissance platoon had been caught off-guard and decimated by enemy sappers who had penetrated the perimeter and blown open a hole for the assault force. The platoon leader and a few others had survived, but most of the men had been killed or wounded. The platoon leader was relieved of his post, but that did little good for the American soldiers lost.

I was not overly concerned about the lack of reinforcement. I was confident of our ability to repel a large-scale enemy attack as long as we made no major blunders. I abided by our long-established aggressive patrolling to prevent the enemy from massing forces close-in for a quick rush on our position, and I continued to push for painstaking discipline in the defense. No, we would not be taken easily; of that I was sure.

But I underestimated the ruthlessness of our enemy. And I failed to realize the extent to which political ideology can displace human morality. It was a major oversight, and it cost us the village of Truong Lam.

The night of December 28 seemed like any other to

me. I sent out the normal patrol a few minutes into dark and checked on the defensive arrangements for the night. Between 2000 and 2200 I catnapped while Platoon Sergeant Palloman began his systematic checks on the readiness of the platoon. At 2220 I counted in the returning patrol. Although they reported seeing nothing, I decided to go out with the next patrol, leaving around midnight. While I waited I decided to sit with a new soldier, Pfc Mark Clements of Des Moines, Iowa, currently manning one of the three machine gun positions.

Clements was a soft-spoken soldier who seemed at ease with his job, not at all nervous in his first combat assignment. Reassured, I lapsed into silence and glanced at the village of Truong Lam below us. It was asleep, the lights all extinguished and the evening conversations ended. How peaceful it seemed. It looked like the town of Bethlehem as I had pictured it as a boy, straw and thatch huts housing people and livestock beneath the twinkling stars.

Content with that thought, I turned again to speak to Clements. The time was approaching 2300 and soon I would have to see that 2d Squad was getting ready for its patrol.

The first explosion ripped one of the huts apart in a blaze of brilliant orange and yellow flame.

"Jeez!" Clements cried out, peering up over the sandbags at the first sight of war he had seen.

"Get your head down, Clements!" I yelled, as I crouched down to await the slashing bullets and fragment shards overhead. I could hear Palloman yelling to the men to get their gear on. We were girding for an attack.

Another deafening explosion, then another, ripped through the night air, punctuated by the staccato clatter of automatic weapons. We braced, trying to pinpoint the direction of attack.

"Sergeant Palloman, what are they aiming at?" I called out. "I can't spot a thing."

Palloman's answer was drowned out by the next explosion. But I didn't need his answer. I realized what was happening at the same time that Lieutenant Thang, the latest in a long line of RF platoon leaders, came screaming up to the wire, pleading for entry.

"My God!" I exclaimed to no one in particular. "They're hitting the village!" It would be a butchery.

Nhan was talking excitedly with Thang. The lieutenant had abandoned his platoon, but they were not the object of the attack. The Viet Cong had penetrated the eastern end of the village and were moving from thatch hut to thatch hut, throwing satchel charges inside and shooting down anything that moved.

I was horrified by the picture forming in my mind. The village would have to become a battlefield. For so long I had avoided that, even at risk to my own men. But I could not avoid it that night. The enemy was destroying the village anyway. I had to fight them on the ground of their choosing or stand by and watch them destroy the village bit by bit. The enemy's tactic was brilliant. I was damned if I fought back and damned if I didn't.

"Sergeant Palloman, leave back 3d Squad and come with me. We're counterattacking into the village in two minutes!"

There was no time to call for artillery illumination. The two squads and the platoon headquarters knelt by the exit through the wire, both Palloman and I poised with hand-held flares. Above the shooting and the screaming in the village, I gave my orders: "Push those VC out of there! Look out for the people—they'll be the ones without weapons. The RF platoon may be alive and fighting. Use your judgment."

I slammed the flare with the palm of my left hand

and Palloman followed suit. We dashed for the village as the flares burst upward. The scene revealed before us was ghastly. A mother ran by me with her decapitated baby, her own left arm hanging by a strip of flesh. Two Viet Cong stood behind her, trying to shoot them down. In a cold rage, I fired into their faces, their heads collapsing into pulpy mush.

First Squad ran by me as Sergeant Palloman swept to the left with 2d Squad. A line of burning huts gave us an indication of how far the Viet Cong had come. Two young girls came running at me, tears of pain streaming from their eyes. At a glance I could see that both had been disfigured by shrapnel.

"Get behind us and wait!" I yelled, half in English, half in Vietnamese. We would tend to them later.

The Viet Cong had their mission—kill as many villagers as quickly as possible—and they were doing it well. But they didn't expect our sudden rush upon them at point-blank range. For a costly moment, they were confused by the onslaught and we ripped their leading edge apart.

But the second wave adjusted and shifted its fire to us. An American rifleman had his hand smashed by an AK round. A second took a blast through his left hip, blood and bone disintegrating in his side. But we rushed in for the kill.

I yelled to Palloman to bring 2d Squad on line with 1st. There had to be some control to our rush so we didn't shoot ourselves up in the melee. Survivors of the RF platoon came to join us.

From somewhere in the smoke and fire a woman emerged with her young son. She thrust the little boy at me, begging for help in Vietnamese. The boy was folded completely in half at the stomach, a deep wound across the small of his back allowing his fat little body to be creased as neatly as a piece of cardboard. Surely he was dead. I looked into the mother's eyes and patted her head. "Later," I said. "I'll help you later."

We pressed the attack back to the edge of the village. Almost a fourth of it was burning now. One more American fell, with a chest wound that collapsed a lung. But we broke the back of the attack; VC bodies lay sprawled on the wire through which they could not withdraw.

I dispatched 1st Squad to continue pursuit out to three hundred meters beyond the village and turned my attention to Truong Lam. The dead and dying lay everywhere amid the burning huts. From the glare of the roaring flames I could see dead and wounded Vietnamese lying in twisted piles. Already the older women had begun their pitiful wails of mourning, shrieking and tearing at their hair and faces. Smoke filled the air, but it could not cover the acrid smell of death that filled my nostrils. Children searched for their missing elders or huddled in groups, groping at each other for comfort, their eyes wide in terror. A mother rocked her one-legged baby to her breast, his lifeless eyes undisturbed by the bright flames silhouetting them both. I set my jaw and turned to my platoon.

The tasks to be performed occurred to me almost mechanically. First, sweep the entire village for remnants of the enemy force. Second, gather up the wounded and arrange for their treatment. Third, insure against an enemy counterattack back into the village or against my lightly manned platoon perimeter. The thought process continued to function, but at the base of it my emotions raged. The worst had happened. The enemy had struck directly against the village and had most assuredly killed and wounded many of their own families. It was unbelievable, but it had been done. The number of enemy dead was moot; the village had been lost. Even as I tended to the wounded, even as I admired the coolness and medical competence of the battalion surgeon and his corpsmen as they worked in the village through the night, I knew that Truong Lam had been a defeat. Like the entire American system in Vietnam, we had fought a limited military war with constrained objectives; the enemy had fought a total political war with no preordained restrictions. We were doomed from the outset.

The village had been the enemy's objective all along. To U.S. forces and to the government of Vietnam, it was a symbol of allied control over the small area of Binh Dinh province, previously a hotbed of Communist domination. To the Viet Cong, the village was a blight on their reputation as the holder of power and the dominant force among the population of Tam Quon district. As long as Truong Lam stood, Viet Cong legitimacy was questioned, and their base of support was in jeopardy.

I had known from the beginning that some, but not all, of the villagers were sympathetic to the Communists. And I also knew that to some, Viet Cong were family—their mothers and fathers, wives, and children. But it was this very fact that made Truong Lam, in my mind, a sanctuary. Our purpose was to keep it a viable entity—alive, healthy, and prosperous. The American platoon was the means to that end. It had nurtured the village, protected it, kept it free of enemy interference. The RF platoon quartered within the village itself was important for its symbolism—it was a Vietnamese force in a Vietnamese village, but it could not preserve the existence of the village as the Americans could.

We were the focus of the Viet Cong attacks because we kept the village alive. If we died, so would the village. But even at that, we were the indirect objective. The village was the direct objective. If the villagers were destroyed, then there could be no village. But only now did I understand that kind of logic.

It had not occurred to me that the enemy could take such a step. To hit the village would insure the wounding and killing of their own kin. In a battle within the confines of the village itself there could be no discrimination among family, Communist sympathizers, and government loyalists. Every day I saw the children of the village. They were like all children—cute, endearing, growing—with the emotional and physical needs of children the world over. I couldn't hurt them. It was unthinkable. The possibility was so barbaric that it was alien to my mind.

But my mind was not the mind of the enemy. Though I had tried to understand them, even to think like them (if only to defeat them), I had fallen short.

In the village of Truong Lam over a score of the inhabitants lay dead. Twice that many were wounded. By dawn, the irreversible exodus began. Grabbing the few belongings they had left, the surviving villagers began their flow out the still-smoldering village gate. They trudged past the shroud-covered bodies, large and small unmoving mounds, their eyes averted stoically, advancing to what they hoped would be less violent ground. Only the relatives of the dead stayed behind to arrange for the burial of their kin.

I stood by the latrine where so often I had been embarrassed by passing villagers. Today I was even more embarrassed; it was an embarrassment born of tragedy, of a sense of having failed them. The one-armed girl walked by, the girl Barnes had wounded long ago. I thought I saw a look of defiance in her eyes. The orphans cared for by the murdered old woman came by, eyes downcast, avoiding my searching look. The woman Nhan had favored walked by with her aged mother. Nhan ignored their passage as he smoked a cigarette and warmed a can of water for his coffee.

Tall palm trees in the eastern distance waved gently against the sea breeze, framed by a clear, blue sky. The lush green of rice paddies and nearby potato fields set a peaceful picture of serene countryside. Only the stench of death properly marked the tragedy of the mournful stream of humanity.

Throughout the morning the numbers of villagers dwindled. As they went, the platoon perimeter became a mockery of what we had fought so many months to hold. By late afternoon, Truong Lam was a ghost town. The well by which the village chief had been shot stood unused, the ground around it soaked with yet-fresh blood from the night before. The tin roofs that Lieutenant O'Brien had died carrying to Truong Lam creaked on burnt supports. Truong Lam was no more.

For a few more days we continued to patrol the area. It was a bureaucratic gesture, a mere continuance of what we had been doing for so long. I kept to myself, my own recognition of the emptiness of our work. It was essential for the men to be convinced of the importance of their mission. Leadership must always be positive.

# EPILOGUE

Shortly after the first of the year, reality caught up with bureaucracy, and the mission of the platoon changed. We would be moving to a new area to try our hand again at wresting control of the population away from the Viet Cong. But I would not be going with the platoon. My time had come. A new lieutenant would take the men on to fresh terrain.

On the last day of my command I gathered up the platoon for a quick snapshot. I wanted to remember those who were there with me at the end. Hurriedly, to avoid presenting a prolonged target to a watching enemy, they gathered in as I snapped the picture. Young faces looking at me, like so many high school boys on an afternoon beer party, out for a lark. As I studied the picture during the following months, their numbers would diminish—some as casualties, some by normal rotation home—until six months later only Phil Nail would remain, the perennial infantryman.

By midmorning the new lieutenant arrived, a big strapping boy, slightly overweight and scared to death of what lay before him. Well he might have been. Twenty-five days later he went home without a leg.

As I briefed him that day on the structure of the platoon and the strengths and weaknesses of the men, I sensed my own mixed emotions of relief and shame: relief at the knowledge that I would be removed from immediate danger; shame at the knowledge that my men would not, and that I could feel relief.

Shortly before the last helicopter of the day came in, I went to each man and said good-bye. They did not seem resentful. Some even said they were glad for me. Their very nobility deepened my remorse.

"Don't worry about me, L.T.," said Nail. "You know I always get over."

Sergeant Palloman clasped my hand firmly. "We'll miss you, sir. We really gave them hell together."

I looked into his steady eyes and felt good knowing he would still be there looking out for the platoon. "Give the new lieutenant all the support you gave me, and this platoon will do just fine. And for God's sake, don't be so damn reckless! Keep your head down."

One by one I made my good-byes. Even at the end I felt the pressure of leadership. I tried to be upbeat, to avoid any semblance of mawkishness, to hide the concerns I had for each man and the shame I felt at leaving them. When it was done, something was missing. It was Killigan. How strange that he was not there to say good-bye. To me he *was* the platoon, epitomizing its resilience, its dedication, its complete commitment. I ran to the waiting helicopter. As we pulled up from the landing zone I could see the platoon perimeter and the abandoned village beneath me. The platoon was scurrying around to prepare for the evening's patrol. The gesture seemed so pointless, juxtaposed beside the gray and empty Truong Lam. Already the vegetation was beginning to encroach on the village boundary as if to blot out the memory of what had happened there. And then the scene disappeared from my view as we turned toward LZ English.

As scheduled, the platoon moved on and continued to fight. As long as I could, I kept a watch on the fate of the men. Specialist Nail was wounded yet again, "got over" for a month in the hospital, and returned to his radio. Platoon Sergeant Palloman got out in front of the platoon in a firefight and took an enemy rocket-propelled grenade in the right leg. With luck he kept his leg, but his fighting days in Vietnam were over. I learned that Corporal Killigan survived his wounds, although he lost a lung and a stretch of his intestines. Sergeant Donne made it home untouched, one of the few. Sergeant James, returning to the platoon again, and Specialist King were killed, although the circumstances surrounding their deaths were never made clear to me.

And so it went. An infantryman's days were numbered, and the law of attrition applied to the platoon as it always did. Had I returned a few days later to the same outfit, I would scarcely have recognized it as the one I left.

In the summer of 1971 I flew out of Camranh Bay to return to my wife and infant son. I had just made captain. It had been a long twelve months, and I had changed in more ways than rank.

My new title did not spare me the humiliation of a drug shakedown. A urine test was given to me, along with every other soldier, the day before departure. In Seattle I was held up for two hours while my bags were thoroughly searched for contraband.

There was no fanfare to greet us as we returned from the war. Once the customs and drug inspections were completed at McChord Air Force Base, we made our own way to the Seattle-Tacoma Airport. No countrymen welcomed us. We might have been coming back from a walk to the corner grocery store. Nor did we have words of farewell for each other as we drifted apart on the West Coast. We were all strangers to one another. No one I went over with came back with me on the plane. My two seatmates on the way over, class-mates from West Point, were dead.

At National Airport in Washington, D.C., a pretty young woman stood waiting in the terminal as I walked up the ramp. By her knee stood a fifteen-month-old child with curly blond hair, barely able to keep his balance on his chubby little legs. I kissed them both hello. The woman was happy; the boy was confused. I was both. I was also sad. I mourned for the men I had left behind. I grieved that their country would never know what fine men they were. I was proud to have served with them.